DON'T WAI[T FOR]
HIM TO TE[LL YOU]

You might think you know your husband.
Mild, meek, content with a tame and
tepid sex life.

Don't you believe it.

Every man has secret desires that he
dreams of satisfying, and a weakness
for the woman who makes those dreams
come true.

Don't wait for him to tell you what those
desires are. He won't. Instead, he'll
yearn for a woman who doesn't have to
be told what to do. A woman who knows
that in bed he is The Lover—not a
husband, a head of the family, a
businessman, a worker. The Lover. And
he wants the woman in his bed to be
The Lover, too.

Let this book show you the way to the
secret lover in your husband and the
secret lover in you. Get your hands on
it before the Other Woman gets her
hands on him!

SEX
SECRETS
OF THE
OTHER
WOMAN

by

Graham Masterton

A SIGNET BOOK

NEW AMERICAN LIBRARY

A DIVISION OF PENGUIN BOOKS USA INC.

NAL BOOKS ARE AVAILABLE AT QUANTITY DISCOUNTS
WHEN USED TO PROMOTE PRODUCTS OR SERVICES.
FOR INFORMATION PLEASE WRITE TO PREMIUM MARKETING DIVISION,
NEW AMERICAN LIBRARY, 1633 BROADWAY,
NEW YORK, NEW YORK 10019.

Ⓢ

SIGNET, SIGNET CLASSIC, MENTOR, ONYX, PLUME, MERIDIAN
and NAL BOOKS are published by New American Library,
a division of Penguin Books USA Inc.,
1633 Broadway, New York, New York 10019

First Printing, October, 1989

1 2 3 4 5 6 7 8 9

PRINTED IN THE UNITED STATES OF AMERICA

You know whom this is for.
There will never be
any other woman but you.

Contents

Prologue

What Has She Got That I Haven't?

You've seen her often enough. The Other Woman. The woman for whom a husband will leave his wife—in spite of the heartache, in spite of the trauma, in spite of the massive expense.

Together, she and the husband look like young lovers, with eyes for nobody else but each other. And you think to yourself, *I hope to heaven that my husband never leaves me for anybody like that.*

She's not always prettier than the wife he left her for. Often—at first sight—the wife and the other woman will look startlingly similar. The husband's friends and colleagues will shake their heads in sheer bewilderment and wonder why he bothered to go through all of the emotional and financial upheaval just to end up with a woman who could easily be mistaken for the woman he left.

Well, there are all kinds of reasons for marriage breakups. Boredom, money worries, a clash of intellectual needs, drinking, irritating personal habits, or a plain and simple growing-apart. But when a man leaves his wife for another woman, the root cause is almost always sexual, in one guise or another.

But if it's sexual, you say, why doesn't the husband leave his wife for the sexiest-looking woman around? The office flirt with the blond hair and the big chest? The young librarian with the melting eyes and the mini-skirts?

Sometimes he does. But an outward appearance

of sexinesss is not always paramount. During sixteen years of extensive personal research into what attracts people to other people—and why—I have discovered again and again that it is not so much a woman's looks that make her sexually magnetic, but her *attitude* toward sex.

What the other women have that the abandoned wives don't have is an ability to be able to excite men in just the way that men like to be excited. To give them a varied and satisfying sex life that never falls off in interest.

A sex life that knows no embarrassment, no deception, and no secretly unfulfilled urges on either side.

A few women have a natural aptitude for pleasing men, an understanding that a man's sexual needs are complicated and multi-layered, and that even a man who seems quite mild-mannered and ordinary may very well have deeply hidden sexual fantasies of startling intensity.

But for most women, satisfying their husbands or lovers is a skill that has to be *learned*—an ability that they can acquire only through self-education and experience.

There is no discredit at all in your not knowing what the man in your life is secretly hankering for. Does he want to take you to bed in black stockings and stiletto heels? Does he want to make love to you in the open air? Would he like to tie you up? You can only know if he tells you, and the chances are that he has some sexual cravings to which he has never confessed, because the truth is that almost *all* men do.

I have files bulging with letters that begin, "I don't know how to explain to my wife that I'd like to . . ."

But if your husband or lover hasn't told you about his secret desires, they can't be all that important, surely?

Wrong! He hasn't told you about them because he's afraid that you'll be shocked, or that you'll think he's perverted or peculiar, or because he's afraid that you'll get the idea that you're in some way inadequate.

Because he's kept his secret desires secret, that doesn't mean for a moment that he doesn't love you, or that he doesn't find you sexually exciting. It simply means that he doesn't know how to tell you what he wants ... and the longer you've been living together, the more difficult it becomes for him to speak out.

Imagine your reaction after nine years of marriage if you suddenly discovered that your husband had always wanted you to wear garters and stockings and a wasp-waisted corset when you went to bed, but had never found the words to tell you.

Would you feel shocked? Embarrassed? Frustrated? Annoyed? Disgusted? Betrayed?

Or would you feel relieved that at last he managed to tell you?

I cannot stress too strongly the importance in a happy and satisfying sex life of knowing what your lover's secret sexual urges are—and doing what you can to satisfy them.

Quite apart from the fact that your sex life could be much more exciting, you should remember that so long as your lover's secret sexual urges remain unfulfilled at home, there will always be the possibility that he will be tempted one day to have them fulfilled elsewhere.

Time and time again I have been asked by bewildered wives, "Why did he go off with a cheap-looking woman like that?" "Why did he go to a prostitute?" "Why did he visit a massage parlor?"

These wives have suddenly—and painfully—discovered a side to their husbands' sexual personality that they had never suspected in all the time they have been together. A side that their husbands were reluctant to reveal because it seemed too shocking, or too extreme.

There are many men whose view of marriage is that their wives are somehow different from other women—pure and sacred. Barrett, thirty-eight, an insurance executive from Indianapolis, told me, "I would never consider asking Jean, my wife, to perform oral sex on me. And I certainly wouldn't do it to her. I just wouldn't. She's my wife, the mother of my children."

Yet Barrett had been carrying on an affair with a secretary in his office for almost eighteen months —an affair in which he expected frequent "sixty-nine" and other sexual variations, including anal intercourse and mutual masturbation.

When I discussed her sex life with Jean, she said she believed that Barrett was fully satisfied with their lovemaking—"although I have to say that our sex is comforting rather than exciting."

Would she consider oral sex if she thought that Barrett would enjoy it?

"I guess so. I've never thought about it. I love him, for sure, and I don't think that anything a man and wife do together in the privacy of the marriage bed is wrong or immoral, except if one partner hurts the other. But I don't think he'd care for it. He's not a very sexual man."

Robert, a forty-year-old computer engineer from Sherman Oaks, California, gave me a similar response to Barrett's. "I live with Velma, we're parents and we're friends. Yes, we make love, certainly we do. But I wouldn't ask Velma to do anything way-out in bed. How could I face her over the breakfast counter in the morning if I'd seen her the previous night with my pecker in her mouth?"

Robert was an intermittent customer at a downtown massage parlor, where he admitted that he paid for oral sex and "relief" massages.

Velma was less liberal in her view of married sex than Jean. But she believed that Robert was "totally content" with their sex life. Would she consider acts of oral sex with him?

"He wouldn't be interested in anything like that."

Would she like to do it?

"If I thought that he really wanted me to. But it's not the kind of thing that wives do, is it?"

Then who does do it?

"Well . . . hookers, I guess."

In his study of the emergence of the permissive society, *Thy Neighbor's Wife,* Gay Talese comments, "There were distinguished stockbrokers and bankers who negotiated with masseuses for fellatio, explaining that this was something their wives refused to do; and there were blue-collar workers who were similarly satisfied by masseuses but admitted this was something they would never ask their wives to do."

Very few of the dozens of wives to whom I talked before I wrote this book even had an inkling of the strong sexual urges that the men in their lives were keeping hidden from them. Despite what their husbands had said about them refusing oral sex, for instance, almost all of the wives claimed that their husbands had never specifically asked them for it: "He never told me, how was I to know?" Nor had their husbands guided them into it, although two or three women remembered occasions when their husbands had put themselves into positions where "his penis was very close to my face . . . and I suppose, looking back on it, he was trying to encourage me to take it into my mouth."

Oral sex came first on the list of complaints about "Things My Wife Doesn't Do for Me in Bed." But in spite of the wide availability of adult sex education, only a very small percentage of wives knew much about sexual variations and lovemaking techniques, and even those wives who had some theoretical knowledge admitted that they had not considered introducing oral sex or mutual masturbation or anything remotely out of the ordinary into their own relationships.

"Richard and I went to see *Deep Throat* together when it was showing at our neighborhood movie theater," said Charmienne, a thirty-six-year-old music teacher from Sacramento, California. "I think it excited us both, and we spent the whole night making love."

Yet had Charmienne attempted "deep throat" herself? Or anal sex? Or any of the sexual variations demonstrated in the film?

"I'm his wife," she told me. "I'm not his whore."

Yet the same afternoon Richard himself told me that in the past eight years he had been sexually unfaithful to Charmienne "six, maybe seven times." These affairs had been "casual, you know, nothing serious, just getting my rocks off." In each case the women with whom he had been unfaithful had been willing to give him oral or anal sex.

"I couldn't ask Charmienne," he said. "She'd just say no."

I found it interesting that in many cases, wives wouldn't have refused to perform out-of-the-ordinary sexual acts if their husbands had only taken the trouble to ask them. But so often the husband *assumed* that his wife would say no—and quite frequently, I suspect, wouldn't have liked his wife to agree.

So when a husband breaks up his marriage because of what appears to be the greater sexual willingness of another woman, he can often be doing his wife a serious injustice. If only he had plucked up enough courage to tell his wife what he wanted her to do for him in bed, he could have had full sexual satisfaction at home—and not felt the need to search elsewhere.

The purpose of this book is to show you how *you* can acquire the exciting sexual talents of other women: how to deal with your husband's reluctance to tell you his secret sexual needs, how to be the woman he fantasizes about, how to preempt any desire he may feel for another woman's touch. In short, this book will tell you how to be the other woman yourself ... so that he doesn't need to go looking any farther for his sexual satisfaction than the marriage bed.

I'm not going to pretend that giving your husband everything he wants is necessarily going to be easy. You're going to have a difficult time overcoming shyness—both yours and his. Yes, men are just as shy about sex as women—often shyer. Many of the techniques and variations and tips that I will give you in this book will seem shocking when you first read them. You will learn about startling oral sex techniques and extraordinary massages and erotic things to wear, not to mention ways to greet your husband when he comes home from work that may well have you saying, "Me! I couldn't possibly do that."

But you can. You can be sexually brilliant without compromising any of your dignity as a woman. You can be the low-down dirtiest lady that your husband ever secretly hankered for, and at the same time retain your integrity, your personality, your femininity. Because there should be nothing that a couple who really love each other can't do for each other—nothing at all, just so long as neither partner feels degraded or humiliated or hurt.

It has always struck me as extraordinary that so many men believe that "dirty" sex is something "you just don't do with your wife." "Dirty" sex is something you do with whores, or something that you fantasize about, but that you never actually attempt.

The top-ten sexual "no's" that I compiled while preparing this book make fascinating reading. They are the ten most popular sexual variations for which men have a secret craving, but which they know—or at any rate feel—that they cannot suggest to their wives or partners. The ages of the men I talked to ranged from eighteen to sixty-three, so there seemed to be very little difference related to age or experience.

The older man of sixty-three is just as keen for his wife to suck his penis as the young man of only eighteen.

When I talked to other women—second wives and mistresses and women who had successfully taken husbands away from established marriages—I found that while their appearance was frequently similar to the men's first wives—their difference in attitude was remarkable. Not only were most of them aware of the sexual desires that their men felt, but they believed that it was an important part of their rôle in the relationship to satisfy those desires.

More than that, they admitted to plenty of secret sexual desires of their own, and believed that it was equally important that their men satisfied them in return.

In other words, their sex lives were far more communicative, and the communication was two-way.

You won't find it at all simple to improve your sexual communication with your partner, particularly if you haven't been used to discussing sex openly. You may discover that your husband has a particular sexual urge, but that he feels ashamed or guilty about it, or that he is reluctant to share it with you.

And to begin with, the chances are that you yourself will be shocked and disturbed when you find out just how lurid some of his secret desires turn out to be. "I thought I knew him so well," wailed one wife when she discovered that her husband wanted more than anything else to dress her up in a topless basque and black stockings.

But overcoming your own reticence about male sexual fantasies is part of the procedure of growing up, of learning how to be sexually mature and creative in bed. Like many of these other women, you will soon discover that what appeared at first to be the most alarming of sexual urges turn out to be completely harmless.

Laura, a thirty-one-year-old Connecticut wife told me, "Jack came back from New York one evening with a red rubber dress that he wanted me to put on. I was horrified. It seemed so perverted. And, of course, I'd never realized that Jack had any interest in rubber. He was very upset, and so was I, and we had a really bad row. But when he was at work the next day, I thought to myself, What's actually wrong with wearing a red rubber dress, if it turns him on? It's not as though he's going to hurt me or do anything aggressive. Completely the opposite, in fact. So when he came home that evening, I was wearing it. That was a turning point in our marriage. It's been truly wonderful ever since. I still wear rubber clothes that he buys me from time to time. I have rubber leggings and a rubber bra with holes for my nipples to poke through. Rubber doesn't excite me personally, but Jack's excitement when I wear it excites me. I don't think there's anything weird about it anymore, and it certainly hasn't taken over our lives. It's just a particular taste, like some people like Italian food and some people don't."

Think about it. Would you wear rubber if you thought it would really turn your husband on? Or do you find the idea of it shocking? Or frightening, perhaps?

Learning about sexual variations takes time and understanding, both from you and from your partner. But the fruits of openly sharing your husband's tastes in sex can be tremendous. Once you have both overcome your inhibitions, you can rediscover the kind of newly met excitement that you might have believed you had lost for good.

While her thirty-three-year-old husband, Leonard, was at work at his San Diego realty office, his twenty-eight-year-old wife, Sandra, discovered in his den a huge collection of pornographic magazines.

"My first reaction was shock. Total shock. I had seen *Playboy* and magazines like that, but I had never seen anything like these. Then I suppose my second reaction was that I felt cheated—almost as if Len had been having sex with another woman. I closed the drawer and sat outside in the yard with a large vodka. I was physically trembling.

"After about ten minutes, though, I went back into the den and took out the magazines and sat on the floor and looked through them. I was pretty sure that Len wasn't really being unfaithful, and I didn't think there was anything wrong with our love life. But I thought that if he wanted to look at magazines like these, there must be something lacking, and I wanted to find out what it was.

"Most of the magazines were nothing more than page after page of naked girls with their legs wide open. Some of the girls were quite pretty, but most of them were average-to-plain. I certainly didn't count any of them as competition as far as looks were concerned, although some of them had really enormous breasts. A lot of them were stretching their vaginas wide open with their fingers so that the camera could see right up inside. Some of them actually had their fingers inside their vaginas, and one young girl had obviously just had sex, because her vagina was filled with come. She was smiling all over her face. I think the smile shocked me more than anything.

"I spent about a half-hour looking through all of these magazines. Once I'd gotten over the initial shock, I began to find them quite sexy, in a way— not because it turns me on to look at other women, but because I could imagine what it must have been like for the models to pose like that.

"I also found it interesting to see what other women's vaginas looked like. Some of them were quite fleshy, with thick outer lips; and others were just like a thin line. I always used to think that my vagina wasn't very attractive to look at, because I have quite prominent outer lips, but when I looked at those magazines, I realized that lots of women had vaginas exactly like mine.

"I also used to be very embarrassed because my vagina got so wet whenever I was turned on. But almost all of the women in the photographs had wet vaginas, and there they were, showing them off to the whole world!

"I guess it was then that I began to have some understanding why Len had bought all these magazines. I never used to let him look at me. I mean, not really look at me with my legs wide open like that. I had never realized it—and I only really began to understand it when I talked to Len later—but men find the sight of women's vaginas really exciting, a terrific turn-on, and most of the time they don't even care who the woman is. There were lots of photographs in Len's magazines where you couldn't even see the woman's face—just a close-up view of a vagina being held wide open by these fingers with long red fingernails."

So what did Sandra do about her discovery?

"First of all, I thought of putting all the magazines back in the drawer and pretending that I'd never found them. But that would have made me just as sneaky and secretive as Len, and what I wanted to do was get this all out in the open. If I was lacking—if I wasn't very good in bed or something like that—I wanted to know about it, so that I could do my best to improve.

"When Len came home, I was sitting on the couch in the living room looking through one of the magazines. He went red as a beet, I have to tell you. But all I said was, 'I wish you'd showed these to me before. They're really sexy.' He muttered something about thinking I wouldn't be interested. The poor guy was really embarrassed. But I told him I thought it must be fantastic, being a nude model, and perhaps he ought to try taking some pictures of me. You know, the same way as the women in the magazines.

"It's a whole lot easier for me to talk about this now, particularly since the whole experience eventually had the effect of liberating me sexually. But at the time it was very difficult. Len was angry and embarrassed. I was shaking like a leaf. But I kissed him and cuddled him and told him that I loved him and that I only would have been upset if he'd been seeing other women for real. That helped us both a whole lot."

That same evening, Sandra posed for several dozen

Polaroid photographs. "We did them in the bedroom. Len stripped down to his shorts and I wore my clinging pink silk nightdress with nothing underneath. I lay back on the bed and lifted the nightdress up and opened my legs. Leonard kept saying, 'I can't believe this, I can't believe this, it's like a dream come true.' I'd never realized how much I could turn him on. It gave me an extraordinary feeling of confidence, you know? And excitement, and happiness, too. It still does, even today. I suddenly realized that I was making his whole sexual fantasy come to life—and taking all the guilt out of it, too.

"I put my hands down between my legs and held open my vagina just like the girls in the magazines. I was so excited I felt like I could hardly breathe. Len took two or three really close-up photographs, and then I stretched myself open even wider. Len's cock was so hard by then that it reared right out of his shorts. I sat up and took hold of it, and I don't think I'd ever felt it so big and hard before. I rubbed it two or three times and he came right away. Some of it squirted right onto my nightdress, but I kept my vagina held wide open with my left hand and gently squeezed the rest of the drops right into it.

"At that time, that was the most—what do you call it?—that was the most blatant sexual thing that I'd ever done. I mean by far.

"Len took more pictures of my vagina all smothered in come. Then he made love to me. That was the first time we'd ever done it twice, just like that. He turned me over onto my side and made love to me from behind, and all the time he was making love to me I could see the Polaroids of my own vagina scattered all over the bed. Just like the magazines. Pink, shining, and beautiful.

"I experienced the most shattering orgasm ever. It was so intense I actually forgot for an instant who I was and where I was. I mean completely. I opened my eyes when it was over and it was just like being born.

"In a way, I guess I *was* born that day. I learned how to please my husband; I learned to be proud of myself sexually; I learned that nothing a husband and wife do together in the privacy of their bedroom is bad or degrading to either of them. In fact, it's totally the opposite. If you knew how strong and loving our marriage is today . . . Well, you wouldn't believe it. We're like young lovers again.

"But none of it would have happened if I hadn't put aside my own feelings of shock and disgust and anger. You know something: there wouldn't be any need for pornography if every wife behaved like a model once in a while. There's nothing shameful or dirty about the female vagina, and there's nothing shameful or dirty about showing it to your husband."

It is interesting to compare Sandra's experience with that of Betty Dodson, the feminist artist, who was convinced that her genitals were abnormal until an enthusiastic lover showed her a stack of 42nd Street sex magazines.

"I was shocked—but interested," she said. "I thought how it must be very degrading for those poor women to pose in underwear, garter belts, black net stockings, and to have to expose themselves like that, but nonetheless I began looking at the pictures. Indeed, there was a cunt just like mine, and another and another. What a relief! In that one session I had found out that I wasn't deformed . . . I was normal and, as my lover said, actually beautiful."

Betty Dodson arranged consciousness-raising sessions at her New York apartment where women could closely examine their own and other women's genitals. "Some were heart-shaped, others resembled shells, wattles, or orchids, and when the pubic hair and the foreskin above the vagina was pulled back, fully revealing the clitoris, many women saw clearly for the first time the feminine center of arousal, and they were surprised to discover that clitorises could vary in size and shape from recessed pearls to protruding bullets."

Later in this book, we'll discuss how you can arrange sexual-awareness sessions with your own friends. But for the moment, let's go back to the difficulties of establishing sexual communication with your husband.

Not all women find themselves able to respond as positively as Sandra. Karen, twenty-seven, from Cleveland, Ohio, told me, "One night Neil told me that he wanted me to wear my black leather boots in bed. Just the black leather boots, nothing else. I wouldn't do it. I thought it was just perverted. We had a terrible argument about it. It almost broke up our marriage. I didn't understand that he'd been trying to tell me for over three years that he wanted me to wear my boots in bed, you know? And this was the first time he'd plucked up the courage."

Fearing a negative response like Karen's, many husbands never even try to tell their wives what they secretly want in bed.

Thus, when a marriage or a long-term relationship breaks up because of another woman, the abandoned partner is frequently left confused and baffled—never knowing what it is that she failed to do. I can't tell you how often I've heard the plaintive cry, "He always said that he was satisfied."

Colette, thirty-two, a grade-school teacher from Omaha, Nebraska, told me, "My first husband John got drunk one evening after a presentation dinner. We argued all the way home in the car and we were still arguing when we got home. He called me all kinds of terrible names. He said I was frigid and useless in bed. He said in seven years of marriage I had never gone down on him once, not once.

"I had always thought that our sex life was good. Maybe not brilliant, maybe the earth didn't always move. John had never told me that he wanted me to go down on him. I did know about oral sex, but I thought it was something that only groupies and prostitutes did. I couldn't believe that John would want *me* to do it. And, well, to be quite honest about it, I didn't totally relish the idea of taking his penis into my mouth. And what would I do if he came?"

Colette tried to comply with John's request for oral sex, but in her words "never got over the fact that he had bottled his feelings up for seven years and resented me for all of those seven years because I hadn't done it." Seven months later their marriage broke up. Colette remarried—and it is interesting to note that she has no reservations about indulging in oral sex with her new husband.

"He loves it, and because he loves it, I've grown to love it. I don't care now if he comes in my mouth; in fact, I find it exciting and satisfying. Yes, I swallow it, because I think he feels that somehow makes the lovemaking complete. Yes, we're very happy, very close."

Mimi, forty-one, a housewife from Indianapolis, Indiana, came home unexpectedly early from shopping one Saturday to discover her husband, Bill, in the garage, where he was supposed to be changing the spark plugs on the family station wagon.

"The garage door connects directly with the kitchen. I put down my shopping on the kitchen counter and went very quietly to the garage door to give Bill a surprise. I don't know why I did it; I don't usually creep up on people. But this time I was glad I did. The garage door was half-open and I could see Bill reflected in the glass of one of the large veranda windows that we take out in summer and store in the garage.

"He was standing with his back against the wagon, and Julie, the young girl from next door, was hunkered down in front of him. Her head was bobbing backwards and forwards, and I couldn't think what she was doing at first. Then I realized that she was giving him what I later learned to call 'head.'

"I have to confess that I stood quite still and watched them for two or three minutes. I had feelings of dread. I suppose every woman does when she sees her husband with another woman. But I also had strong feelings of curiosity. Here was this young girl performing a sexual act on my husband that I had never performed in the whole of our married lives—never even thought about performing. Yet he was obviously enjoying it. I could hear him saying, 'Yes, yes, yes!' over and over again.

"And what aroused even greater curiosity in me was the fact that Julie was obviously enjoying what she was doing. Her head was bobbing so far forward that she must have been swallowing almost his entire penis, if I can put it like that; and I could see quite clearly in the reflection that she had tugged her skirt right up to her waist, and that she was, well, rubbing herself."

Mimi went back and slammed the kitchen door loudly and called out, "I'm home!" And when Bill emerged from the garage to greet her, he was flushed but welcoming, and it was obvious that Julie hadn't been able to complete her sexual act.

Mimi said, "I didn't feel jealous. I don't know why. I should have, I suppose. But then I didn't believe that Bill would risk leaving me for the twenty-year-old girl next door, as pretty as she was. What really concerned me was that he had obviously felt that I wasn't enough for him, that I didn't do everything in bed that he liked. If anything, I felt determined not to let it happen again.

"Much later that evening, when I was brushing out my hair, Bill came into the dressing room and stood beside me talking. Without any warning, I opened his pajamas and took out his penis. I kissed it and then I took it into my mouth. Bill was so startled he couldn't even speak. I had never done it before, and I think I sucked him far too hard. But he went stiff immediately. He swelled up so big that he filled up my whole mouth. He gripped my shoulders and said, 'No, you mustn't, Mimi, you mustn't!' But he made no attempt to pull away from me. I kept on sucking him and rubbing him until he began to tremble and I knew that he was getting close to a climax. I lost my nerve a little then. I wasn't at all sure that I could actually take his semen into my mouth. So I pressed his penis against my lips, kissing it and licking it with just the tip of my tongue, and rubbing him hard with my hand, and he ejaculated over my lips. His semen was very thick, very warm, and oddly tangy. You remember, of course, that I had never ever tasted it before. I rubbed his penis from to side to side across my lips, kissing it and licking it. I felt tremendously pleased with myself. In fact, I was quite delirious.

Before we went to sleep that night, I told Bill, 'I'm your wife. I love you. If you want me to make love to you in any particular way, don't hide it. Don't lie to me. We can learn together, and then we'll both be happy.' "

Mimi was a wise woman: willing to experiment, willing to take a chance, willing to understand that her husband had sexual urges she had failed to satisfy—not because she didn't want to, not because they disgusted her, but because she simply hadn't known about them.

"I must have been naïve," she said later. "I talked to some of my friends about 'head,' and they all said that their husbands loved to have oral sex. Not all of them enjoyed doing it. Some of them didn't like swallowing the semen. But one or two of them had found a way around that particular problem in different ways. One of my friends said that she wrapped her hair around her husband's penis when she felt that he was close to coming. Apparently he loved the sensation of it, and she found it very exciting to have him ejaculate into her hair."

Other wives told me that their husbands were almost always satisfied at the conclusion of oral sex if they could ejaculate over their faces. "He loves to see the sperm stuck to my eyelashes."

Climaxing over women's faces is an act that is depicted frequently in pornographic videos and magazines. When I edited *Penthouse Forum* magazine, pictures like these used to excite strong opposition from some of the feminists on the editorial staff. "How could a beautiful woman allow herself to be photographed with her face covered in semen? How could any woman allow any man to do that to her?"

But in talking to couples for this book, I found again and again in couples who practiced oral sex with any regularity that the husband perceived the act of climaxing over his wife's mouth or face as a tribute to her beauty, not as an abuse of it, and that the wife saw her acceptance of his tribute as one of the strongest demonstrations of her love for him. In the final analysis, the beauty of any sexual act has very little to do with what a couple is doing physically. It has everything to do with love and with the desire that the couple is trying to express for ultimate intimacy.

You may already have been shocked or disturbed by some of the sexual urges that we have discussed in this prologue. Your reaction is normal and understandable. Although sex books are on sale almost everywhere—and there are endless articles about sex and courtship in women's magazines—almost all of them are impossibly coy, even the ones that claim to be "frank and open" about sexual variations and techniques.

The secret sexual desires that are harbored by almost every man are hardly ever discussed in practical detail, even though they are the principal source of sexual problems in marriage and long-term relationships.

Hedda, a thirty-two-year-old housewife from White Plains, New York, said, "My first husband, Jeff, and I were divorced after seven years of marriage because of Jeff's adultery with a secretary from his office, a girl called Kay. I met him by accident in Macy's about a year after our divorce, and we had coffee together. I asked him what it was about Kay that had really appealed to him so much. And do you know what he said? I couldn't believe what I was hearing at first. He said, 'I asked her never to wear any panties and so she didn't.'

"And do you know, I suddenly remembered a time about two years after we were married when we were invited along to a company picnic. We were very much in love then, we didn't have eyes for anybody else. And while I was getting dressed, he said to me, 'Don't wear any panties when you go to the picnic.' I said to him, 'Are you serious?' And he said to me, 'Sure, I'm totally serious. Don't wear any panties. In fact, it would be fantastic if you never wore panties ever again.'

"I asked him why. But all he could say was he liked the idea of my walking around wearing nothing but my summer dress while he was the only person who knew that I was naked underneath. I said that was ridiculous and embarrassing, and I was quite upset. Supposing my dress was blown up by the wind and everybody saw? It would make me feel cheap, like a prostitute or something. I felt threatened, if you can understand what I mean—as if the man I had married had turned out to be some kind of pervert.

"We had an argument. I remember that he accused me of being frigid. But after that, I forgot all about it and he never asked me again. In fact, he never asked me to do anything unusual for him again. Our love life after that was completely average, completely ordinary. I thought it was quite satisfying, but Jeff had obviously been thinking about women without panties all these years, and Kay was prepared to walk around without panties for him, so that was that."

Kay herself said, "I don't mind leaving off my underwear. I don't go without it all the time, but if we go to a party or out to dinner, I usually do, because I know that it turns him on to think of me sitting next to people talking to them and all the time they don't know what he knows: that I'm naked underneath. Occasionally we'll meet in the kitchen at a dinner party, or else we'll be sitting at the theater, and he'll slip his hand up my dress and stroke me. No, I don't think that's perverted at all. He's crazy about me, and that turns me on, too. It's not panties he's interested in. He doesn't steal underwear from clotheslines or anything like that. He's interested in *me,* and in the sexiness of our relationship.

"There are lots of other things that Jeff likes us to do that he never did with Hedda. When we first went out together, he used to adore making love in the open air, in a field, in the back of the car, on the beach, anyplace at all. He used to be mad for anal sex, too. I didn't like that too much, and I still don't, but I never stopped him doing it; and these days he scarcely ever wants it. Sex is something you share, you know. Women want loving and security and to feel like a queen. Men like black stockings and big breasts. Women have to understand that to get what they want, they're going to have to give men what men want."

In this book, you will discover what it is that men want most out of a sexual relationship. It's not all "black stockings and big breasts." It's not all way-out sex. Men need security and affection and cosseting just as much as women. They need to be seduced, too. As they grow older, they also need to be reassured that they are still sexually attractive.

Actress Patricia Neal, whose thirty-year marriage to novelist Roald Dahl was broken up by Other Woman Felicity Crosland, recently said, "There are *tons* of us—women abandoned after many years of what they thought was happy marriage. In mid-life, the man wants to see how irresistible he still is to younger women. If this works, the older woman, like me, gets kicked out. It's very tough. How they turn their hearts to stone and more or less commit a murder of their marriage, I don't know. But they do."

I can give you no guarantees that what you will learn in this book will give you cast-iron protection against your partner's need for sexual reassurance from other women. But what it will do is give you the knowledge and the wherewithal to understand his sexual needs—from the simplest to the most extreme.

Some of his sexual urges you may not wish to satisfy. That's your decision. But before you decide, it's important that you know what they are, and that you think about them rationally—not in a state of shock, or hurt, or disgust.

Mary, a forty-two-year-old divorcée from Milwaukee, Wisconsin, told me, "When it finally came to the breakup of our marriage, Ron went through a whole list of things that I hadn't done for him. Sexual things, mainly. I was hurt and I was astonished. He had never given me the slightest indication in eighteen years of living together that he wanted things like that. At least, he hadn't made it clear to me. I was very ignorant about sex when I married him. He was the first man I ever slept with. My mother had explained about intercourse and making babies, and I just assumed that intercourse and making babies was all there was to it.

"How was I supposed to have known that he wanted me to put my hand in his pants and masturbate him when he was watching television, and give him oral sex, and that every time he came home for lunch from the office he didn't want my special egg-and-tuna salad; he wanted me to be lying on the couch waiting for him in a see-through nightdress?

"Some of the things on his list sounded plain disgusting at the time. One of his bitterest complaints was that I had never let him watch me go to the bathroom. I was totally shattered by that. It had never even dawned on me that anybody would want to watch anybody else go to the bathroom. And the only time he had ever suggested watching a sexy video—and the terrible part about it was that I couldn't even remember doing this—I had laughed at him.

"I think I was just like tens of millions of other

women. The evidence of what turns men on is all around us. We see the sexy magazines; we see the sexy advertisements; we see wet-T-shirt contests and the bump-and-grind girls at Las Vegas. But either we turn a blind eye to it, or else we delude ourselves that *our* husbands wouldn't be interested in anything like that. We busy ourselves with raising our kids or baking our pies or chasing our careers, and we completely fail to understand that however distasteful we think these pinups and these striptease girls are, they turn men on, they turn our own husbands on. Sex isn't disgusting or horrible, no matter what you do. It's only disgusting and horrible when your partner does it with somebody else, and you lose him, and your marriage breaks up.

"Sure, my marriage broke up through my husband's unwillingness to tell me what he wanted. But it also broke up because of my complete sexual ignorance, because I never understood that sometimes men want their wives to act like whores. Sometimes my husband wanted me to act like a whore, but I never did.

"Of course, I know some women who could never bring themselves to act like that. But there's still plenty of exciting things they could do, like dress a little sexier and show their husbands that they really want to make love.

"Let me tell you something, what happened to Ron and me, that's never going to happen to me again. I've found another man, Howard. He's two years younger than me, and I've been reading all the how-to books that I can lay my hands on." (Mary had written to me after reading *More Ways to Drive Your Man Wild in Bed.*)

Mary vowed, "I'm going to do things to Howard that he didn't even know that he wanted to do."

In this book—through the experiences of real women—you'll learn those sexy secrets that make other women more attractive to men. You'll learn how to apply your newfound knowledge to your own sexual relationship, and how to ensure just as much as any woman can that the man in your life wants to *stay* the man in your life. You can be more exciting than any other woman he's ever likely to meet.

You'll learn how to discover your partner's hidden secret urges, how to anticipate them, how to discuss them with him. You'll learn how to satisfy them, too.

There's no need for you to be worried that your partner might have an urge to do something that you find a total turnoff. Most of the time, your partner won't actually want to act out his most extreme sexual fantasies for real. They're more exciting as they are—as fantasies. After all, you yourself might have a fantasy about being forced to make love to twenty sweaty Roman gladiators, but you wouldn't be too happy if they turned up at your front door with the intention of carrying it out for real.

Just talking about your partner's erotic fantasies is often more than enough, and it can be a very stimulating experience in itself. It can encourage more communication between you while you're actually making love, and you can actually join in each other's wildest sexual daydreams.

Anne, thirty-seven, from Kansas City, Missouri, said, "One night we came back from a pretty boozy party, and when we were in bed, I told Phil that I had often had a fantasy about being nude at a men's club dinner with all these men dressed in white tie and tails, and how they spread me out on the dining table and did things to me. So Phil told me about this fantasy that he'd had, about having a houseful of naked serving girls who would do absolutely everything for him. We talked and talked. It was the first we'd ever talked about our sexual fantasies like that. It was liberating, and it was exciting, and now when we go to bed and make love, we kind of enter into each other's fantasies and describe new things that we could do to each other."

Whatever you discover from this book, and from the sexual experiences with your partner that could follow, I hope that you'll also discover a great deal about yourself as a woman, as a wife, and as a lover (and not necessarily in that order).

I hope you'll find that you get much more sexual satisfaction, too.

Discovering more about sex is always a voyage of adventure. Some people find it frightening, some people find it shocking. But, ultimately, there's nothing at all for you to be frightened about, and nothing at all for you to be shocked about, because we're exploring the outer limits of pleasure and intimacy, and we're looking for nothing more alarming than happiness, and I'll be here to guide you.

If you find anything in this book that takes your breath away, all you have to do is to put the book down and give yourself some time to think about it. Because there is no sexual act described here that can possibly degrade you or dishonor you, if both you and your partner enter into it with no feelings for each other but mutual respect and affection.

You'll find, I hope, that you discover yourself, too, and that you can be your partner's other woman before another woman ever has the chance.

1

I Think Sexy . . .
Therefore I Am Sexy

Positive thinking has successfully been applied to almost every activity you can think of, from selling brushes to flying to the moon.

But there are few fields of human endeavor in which positive thinking bears fruit so promptly and so abundantly as the field of sexual relations.

One small positive thought can improve your sex life—radically, and for good. One decision made in mid-cookie-baking one afternoon that when he comes home tonight things are going to be *different,* things are going to be exciting—coupled with the will-power and the nerve to carry that positive thought right through to its conclusion—that one decision can mean the end of flat, uninspired lovemaking—that one decision can mean an end to the tedious "hullo, dear, what kind of day did you have?" routine.

That one decision—your decision—can signal the beginning of a revived marriage, and a sparkling new life.

Think I'm exaggerating? This is Margaret, a thirty-two-year-old designer from New Rochelle, New York. After three years of living with her boyfriend Michael in New York's Greenwich Village, Margaret became pregnant with their first child, and so they decided to buy a house out of town.

"From the first week we moved out of the city, our marriage started to become routine. I guess it had to take on some kind of regular framework, in a way, because Michael had to take the train into the city every morning and then take it out again every evening. We loved the house, we loved the neighborhood, but somehow the spontaneity went out of everything. We couldn't meet each other for lunch at a moment's notice; we couldn't go to the theater without planning it weeks ahead. And Michael's attitude toward me changed. Because I was no longer involved in the daily life of the city, because I was no longer stimulated in the same way that he was, I guess in his eyes I began to appear dull.

"More and more, he began to treat me like 'the little woman.' We used to be equals. We used to be partners. We used to be friends. We weren't even married yet, and he was treating me like a frumpy wife.

"He would come home, have two martinis, say, 'What a goddamned awful day,' eat the supper that I had prepared for him, without even tasting it, I swear. Then he would read a book or finish off some extra work, and that would be the end of our evening.

"One evening, I kid you not, he didn't even look at me.

"Our love life fell to pieces. We'd always been sexy and physical together. We'd spent quite a few of those city lunchtimes in bed, rather than eating. But now we made love once or twice a week, that's all, sometimes not for weeks at a time. Occasionally —once he'd slept off his exhaustion—Michael would wake up horny in the middle of the night and fuck me very violently. More often than not, he would have finished before I woke up, and I used to find myself smothered in wet, frustrated, angry, my stomach hard as a drum, feeling as if he'd invaded me and disturbed my baby, too.

"One day when I was about five months pregnant, I got bored with the work I was doing, customizing some fussy woman's kitchen for her, and so I dressed myself up and took the train to the city. I was going to give Michael a surprise, take him for lunch at P.J. Clarke's. But as I was crossing the street toward his office building, I saw him coming out of the front door with a pretty young woman. They weren't holding hands or anything, but they were obviously attracted to each other and they were laughing about something.

"I changed direction crossing the street so that they wouldn't see me. Then I hailed a cab and went straight back to the station and caught the train home. As soon as I closed the front door behind me, I burst into tears. I felt terrible. You know, fat and ugly and discarded, like a used pair of shoes.

"When I got home I went straightaway to see my next-door neighbor, who had always been very supportive and friendly. She said that her first marriage had broken up when she was pregnant. It was a whole lot to do with the woman concentrating all of her attention on the coming child, and the man suddenly feeling left out. She guessed that Michael probably wasn't cheating on me, but he was courting other women because they flattered him and made him feel like he was the center of attention.

"My neighbor gave me one piece of really sound advice. She said that I shouldn't start resenting Michael and that I shouldn't be overdefensive about the baby. It was his baby, too, I should help him to share the experience, sexually as well as every other way.

"I spent a long time thinking about Michael and what I should do. It had to be something that I wanted to do, something that turned me on, too; otherwise I was just beging more of a slave to the situation than before.

"When I was about fourteen, I had read a letter in a woman's magazine about housewives who spent all day in the nude ... doing their housework in the nude, everything ... I think they had a name for it, like 'jaybirding.' Well, for some reason that has also appealed to me, but I had never quite plucked up the courage to try it. But about two days later, I tried it. I didn't wear anything all day, except when I went to the supermarket to buy some chicken pieces, and then I wore nothing but a shift dress, nothing underneath it, and I took it off as soon as I got home. I cleaned the house in the nude, I cooked supper in the nude. It was very erotic in a quiet way, and very liberating, too.

"That evening when Michael came home, I was still nude. He couldn't believe his eyes. I kissed him and took off his coat and told him to come straight upstairs to bed. He said, 'No martini?' I'll always remember that. I said, 'No martini,' and took him to bed.

"The difference was that I was already sexually aroused because I'd spent all day naked, thinking about what I was going to do. And *I* made love to him. I loosened his necktie and unbuttoned his shirt and unbuckled his belt.

"He was so hard that his boxer shorts were rearing up. He tried to get up, to take control of the situation, but I pushed him gently back on to the bed and tugged down his shorts, and then I lay next to him and kissed him on the lips and slowly massaged his cock at the same time, very slowly, and told him that I had been naked all day waiting for him and daydreaming about him. He couldn't figure out what on earth had gotten into me, but he liked it all the same!

"I liked it, too. That was the very first time that I had taken charge of our lovemaking, and I was doing what I wanted to do, at my speed. Michael had always been so quick in bed, so frantic, as if he was bursting to come and couldn't wait. Well, that afternoon I made him wait.

"It was beautiful. The sun was shining through the bedroom curtains; the day was really warm and quiet. We could hear people talking outside. Michael tried to get up again, but again I pushed him back. I knelt over his legs and leaned forward and massaged his cock between my breasts.

"Of course, my breasts were very much bigger then, because I was pregnant. Michael adored it. At last he lay back and let me take control. I squashed my breasts close together with my hands, with his cock pressed between them, so that he was actually making love to my cleavage. His cock began to get wet and slippery at the top, so I rubbed it against my nipples. My nipples were so stiff that when I stretched open the hole at the end of his cock, I could actually push my nipples halfway inside.

"I was playing, I was experimenting. I had never had the time or the opportunity before. I was finding out about sex for the first time, believe it or not. But I had to do it at my own speed. I had to be positive about it.

"In the end I carefully sat on top of Michael and guided his cock up inside me. I preferred to sit on top of him, because that meant I had complete control over how far up his cock went. He couldn't ram it into me, like he usually did. I felt so much more at peace about making love to him like this. I mean, this was making love, not being used as a convenient hole. For the first time I had that beautiful feeling that every woman should have when she makes love to her husband during pregnancy. I had the baby inside me, I had my husband's cock inside me, both together, we were lovers and a family all at once.

"I moved gently up and down on Michael's cock, and the feelings it gave me were like nothing I had ever felt before. I could reach behind me and cup his balls in my hand and gently squeeze them. I could feel where he and I were joined, the hardness of his cock sliding in and out of the softness of my vagina. I really luxuriated in it. I climaxed, and then he climaxed. We hadn't come so close together for years. We hadn't felt so close together for years, even when we were trying for the baby. There was no shame or embarrassment or self-consciousness between us at all. We lay together side by side while the sun gradually went down, and we kissed, and a little later we made love for a second time.

"Michael said, 'I never knew that making love

could be so fantastic.' And he came home an hour early the following day, and I was naked then, too.

"That was the beginning of my new marriage. We still have arguments, we still have down days. But, then, everybody does. That's part of being married. But when I was thinking about it the next day, it occurred to me that literally millions of women must go through their whole married lives never even knowing what really exciting lovemaking is all about, because their husbands certainly don't know, and they never have the courage to say, 'Hey, let's slow down here, let's share our lovemaking,' you know? I mean, Michael wasn't a chauvinist or anything like that, but he had the same idea as so many men: that women are there for their sexual convenience, what women feel about sex doesn't matter. At its worst, what millions of husbands do to their wives is practically rape, and at its best it's not much more than masturbation.

"I believe women have to think positive about their sex lives. I believe they have to make a conscious effort to stop being ashamed or embarrassed about their sexual feelings. I believe they have to realize that most men are not very knowledgeable about sex—and not very good at it, either. I mean, how can they be? I believe that once both men and women realize that and try to learn about sex together, so many marriages will come back to life again. I know mine did."

I have quoted from Margaret's interview at length because it highlights a situation in which countless young wives find themselves when they become pregnant. There are no exact statistics available, but a very high percentage of marriages break up during and immediately after pregnancy; and the steps that Margaret took to make sure that she and her husband not only stayed together but actually improved their sex life show that positive sexual thinking can be of enormous importance through any particularly sensitive times in your relationship with the man in your life.

Incidentally, lovemaking during pregnancy is usually quite safe, but it's worth asking your physician about it. You should avoid fierce thrusting sex like Michael's; and if you enjoy oral sex, you should refrain from swallowing semen, particularly during the late stages of your pregnancy, since it contains enzymes that can contribute to bringing on early labor.

Apart from your pregnancy, there are many other sexually sensitive moments in a man's life.

- When he reaches the age of thirty.
- When he's going through severe stress at work, or if he loses his job.
- When you move.
- When (and if) he has a vasectomy.
- When he reaches the age of forty.
- When he's promoted at work.
- When he realizes that younger girls are attracted to mature and confident men.
- When your children start bringing pretty young girlfriends home.
- When your children all leave home.
- When he reaches the age of fifty.
- When he can no longer compete at strenuous sports.
- When he reaches retirement age.
- When he finds his sexual performance isn't what it was when he was younger.

At all of those sexually sensitive times, a man is three times more susceptible to the enticements of other women (just as, indeed, a woman at her sensitive times can be equally susceptible to the flattery of other men).

Those are the times when you need to make a special effort to think sexy, and to be sexy ... to make him feel that he's sexually attractive and a good lover and that you're the foxiest lady that he's ever going to meet.

At times of disappointment or fear or stress, he

will be tempted by women who will offer him a shoulder to cry on and reassurance that he's still a man with a capital M. You'll say to him, "Oh stop grumbling, darling, everything's going to turn out okay."

She'll say to him, "You poor thing, nobody understands you how brilliant you are, but I do."

You'll sit up in bed reading a book, believing that your lovemaking will resume when he's gotten over his problems. She'll kiss him and put her arms around him and stroke him into arousal even when he doesn't feel like it.

You'll say, "Feeling more cheerful today, dear?" She'll say, "I want you, you horny ram." Or words to that effect.

At times of achievement, the other woman will give him all the flattery that you think he deserves, and more. You'll say, "At last they appreciate you." She'll say, "Take me to bed . . . now." She will make him feel powerful and successful and she will convince him that his power and his success have enhanced his sexual prowess, too.

Using sex as a way to sympathize with a man—or as a way to congratulate him for his achievements—is one of the key ways in which other women attract your husbands and lovers. Whether a man has failed or succeeded, they make him feel better as a man. Still virile, if he's suffered a setback. Even more manly, if he's scored a success.

Many women still fail to understand that a man's response to sexual stimuli is almost instantaneous. A man can flick his eyes at the cover of a sexy magazine, or catch the briefest glimpse of a woman's breast as she leans across a table to hand him a cup of coffee. His arousal can be immediate, and before you can say Hägar the Horrible, he can be physically ready to have intercourse. That is, erect and aroused.

But at the same time, men frequently have difficulty in initiating a sexual approach. They're shy, or they're clumsy, or they're not sure whether the woman they're interested in wants to have sex with them or not, or how to persuade her to have sex if she's not immediately responsive.

So, the women who score are the women who can recognize when a man is interested in them and who can help him to say the right things to get them both into bed. And that is why your best defense against other women is to think sexy day and night, and to be sexy day and night—remembering that your man is still a man and that his attention can be attracted by the slightest revelation of inner thigh, the least flirtatious gasp, the tiniest moment of eye contact.

No sexual relationship is safe, in the sense that both partners can promise that for the rest of their lives they will never be attracted by anyone else. No sexual relationship worthy of the name ought to be safe. Sexual relationships that are safe are dull and unstimulating, and will give joy to neither partner.

If you want to keep your sexual relationship stimulating and exciting—and thereby increase the chances of it lasting into erotic old age—you can't leave it to your husband or lover to make all the first moves. Sandy, a twenty-three-year-old divorcée from San Juan Capistrano, California, told me, "Phil never tried to make love to me any place else but the bedroom, at night, and then it was all over before I knew it. After eight weeks of marriage, I began to think that there was something sexually wrong with me, that my body was peculiar. When he was at work, I used to look at my cunt in the mirror, trying to decide if it was particularly ugly or not. Then one evening about five months after we married I caught him at a party, making love to this strange girl in the kitchen. He was sitting on the counter with his pants around his ankles and she was sitting on top of him with her dress pulled up, bouncing up and down like the Lone Ranger. I turned around and walked straight out. Phil didn't even see me. But when we left the party, I told

Phil that was it, that was the end of our marriage, I wanted a divorce. He said he wasn't surprised, because I'd never wanted sex. I couldn't believe what he was telling me. I said, 'Me? Never wanted sex? It was you who never gave it to me!' But he said, 'How was I to know what you wanted? You never gave me the slightest indication.' "

Sandy's story seems incredible, but again and again in the letters I received from readers during my years at *Penthouse* and *Forum*, and in the fifteen years of sexual research I have undertaken since then, I have come across variations of the same story. I have talked to literally scores of wives whose husbands make love to them so seldom that they have come to believe (quite wrongly) that they are plain or sexually unattractive. Especially since—when it does happen—their lovemaking is almost always quick and impersonal and perfunctory.

And I have come across scores of husbands who are firmly convinced that their wives are impossibly frigid, just because their wives never take the initiative in bed and rarely show any overt interest in sex. "She never touched me, she never put her arm around me. Just once, if she'd turned over in bed and put her hand on my cock, I would've known that she was interested. But she never did, in nine years of marriage, not once. It was always up to me to make the first move, and how was I to know whether she felt like it or not?"

Night after night, all over the nation, couples are lying next to each other, needing each other, wanting each other, yet unable to communicate their desire by word or by gesture. A greater tragedy of noncommunication happens every night in this nation's marriage beds than all the years of the Cold War put together.

It's caused mostly by lack of knowledge about sex, and in particular by men's lack of knowledge about women and women's lack of knowledge about men.

With a lack of knowledge, naturally enough, comes

a lack of confidence. And that lack of confidence makes it even harder for men and women to tell each other what they need.

"When we were divorced, my ex-wife told the court that I scarcely ever made love to her and that I had never satisfied her. I was shattered. I had always believed that she didn't care for sex very much. She never talked about sex, never made any demanding suggestions. It was like listening to a totally different woman, a woman I didn't even know."

It's impossible to say by how much the divorce rate could be reduced by better sexual communication. But there is no question that millions of potentially happy marriages are marred forever by nothing more dramatic than the inability of husbands and wives to discuss their sexual needs together.

Women who do appreciate men's sexual needs and who are willing to satisfy them will always come out best—especially at those sensitive times when a man is very vulnerable to outside attractions.

Now you might well say—as several women *have* said to me, and with considerable vehemence—that it is your husband's duty to find out about sex and take the full responsibility for improving your sex life. "When I married him, I expected him to guide me and teach me. I didn't realize that he didn't know any more about sex than I did." "Why doesn't he ever suggest anything different, like making love in front of the fire drinking wine and listening to music? I know that he'd enjoy it, but I'm not going to suggest it if he's not. It's up to him." "Why should I wear the sexy underwear and striptease for him? Why doesn't he ever do anything like that for me?"

If you feel that your husband's or lover's sex technique could use some brushing-up, you could suggest to him that he read some informative books about sex. That's if you feel he can handle such a suggestion without taking offense.

With many men, you could be running the risk of making them feel that they are somehow sexually inadequate, or that you are dissatisfied with their sexual performance. This might very well be true (63 percent of U.S. women think their sex partners are "lacking"). But men are very prickly when it comes to casting doubts on their virility and their skill in bed, and the least helpful begining for your new revitalized sex life would be an out-and-out row.

You could also seriously damage his sexual confidence, and that wouldn't do you any good at all.

If you suspect that your man will react badly to an outright proposal that he bone up on his basic sex education, then there are many ways in which you can improve your sex life quickly and effectively and without a ferocious confrontation.

The first, as we have seen, is to sit down and ask yourself what you want from your sex life and what you think your partner wants from his sex life.

Don't allow yourself to feel resentful about your man's lack of sensitivity and skill. Make a positive decision that if he won't improve his sex technique on his own, then you're going to do it for him.

You're going to take charge of your sex life, even though he'll never know it. All he'll ever know is that he feels much sexier, much more virile, much more satisfied.

That, after all, is one of the greatest attractions of other women. They have the knack of making men feel better in bed.

Of course, every couple's sexual relationship is different and suffers from different problems.

Here's Susan, the twenty-four-year-old wife of a physics professor at a famous midwestern university. It would identify her too easily to name it.

"Pretty often, when I was dressing in the morning, David would watch me and say that he thought I looked sexy with no T-shirt on, just my jeans, with my breasts bare. I used to laugh and feel embarrassed. I always used to think that my breasts were too big, and you wouldn't catch me bouncing around topless.

"But about six months ago I was having coffee with a friend of mine at our local bookstore and I happened to see David passing the window with a couple of his students. One of them was a girl around nineteen, very pretty, dark like me, with very big breasts and a skimpy sleeveless top, and when I watched David talking to her, it was obvious that he found her attractive.

"My friend noticed, too, that's how obvious it was. 'Looks like you've got competition,' she told me. All I did was laugh about it. Well, what could I say? But I spent the rest of the week with a picture of David and that girl going around in my mind, and it did worry me and make me feel jealous, and because I felt jealous, I was bad-tempered, and that didn't help things at all.

"On Saturday afternoon he said he had to take some of his students for a special class, and I went crazy because he was supposed to take me to the supermarket. We had a terrible argument. David said I bitched all the time. I told him to go to hell. In the end he agreed to take me, but it was awful, both of us sulked the whole afternoon.

"The next morning, though, I got up early to make some breakfast. David was still asleep because he'd been up late the night before, grading papers. I put on my jeans, but the T-shirt I wanted to wear was still downstairs in the laundry room. So I went downstairs topless.

"I saw myself in the mirror, and stopped, and remembered what David had said. I thought: Susan, you have to stop acting jealous. Be positive. If David's attracted to a busty young girl, ask yourself why. Maybe he's not getting at home what he's getting in the classroom, and that's flirtation and sexiness and plain old admiration.

"I asked myself, If I walk around bare-breasted all day, David's going to love it—but am I going to love it? I mean, my philosophy about marriage has always been, what's good for the goose is good for the gander. Everything has to be mutual.

"As you can see, I'm quite big-breasted. I guess that's one of the reasons that David was attracted to me in the first place. But it can be uncomfortable, going without a bra. But I thought, No, I'll try it. It feels okay. In fact, it feels quite sexy.

"So I made us some breakfast and took it up on a tray, along with the Sunday paper. David had already woken up, and when I came in, he smiled and said good morning, and then he said, 'I hope we've gotten over yesterday.' I said, Sure, and sat on the bed and poured some coffee and spread some toast and started reading the funnies.

"After a while, David said, 'I can't stand this any longer.' I said, 'What?' And he said, 'You dressed like that. You're driving me crazy.'

" 'Oh,' I said, playing very innocent. 'Do you like it?'

"He said, 'Like it? I've got the Sears building under this blanket!'

"He climbed out from between the covers, naked, and he pushed me back on to the bed. He kissed my lips and squeezed my breasts, and all the time he was whispering into my ear how sexy I looked and how much he loved me. He took my left breast in both hands, really cupping it, and he bent forward and kissed my nipple and nipped it gently with his teeth until it was standing out stiff and hard like a baby's finger. Then he did the same with my right breast.

"At last he wrenched open my jeans and tugged them down to my knees. Then he turned me over so that I was bunched up on the bed with my bottom in the air, and he put his hands around and felt the weight of my breasts, and said, 'You're fabulous. You're absolutely fabulous. You have the most beautiful breasts, and you should never cover them up, ever.'

"This time I wasn't embarrassed and I didn't say anything stupid in reply, like 'I can't go shopping topless, can I?' which is the kind of thing I used to say before. David was making love to me, he had a fantasy, and the terrific thing was that I was his fantasy, I was doing what he had always wanted me to do.

"I could hardly move because of my jeans tight around my knees, but David opened up my pussy with his thumbs and then he pushed his stiff cock right into me.

"It was incredible. It was probably my imagination, but I thought that I had never ever felt him so stiff. He seemed enormous, and I could feel the bump of his head going in and out between the lips of my pussy. He moistened his fingers between my legs and then he reached forward and massaged my nipples with my own juice, tugging them and twisting them until they absolutely tingled.

"I reached down with one hand and cupped his balls, gently rolling them. I had never done that before, either, and I could hear him suck in his breath. I knew that he couldn't be far away from having a climax. His balls felt very tight, and he was pushing himself into me more and more jerkily, as if he was gradually losing control. I played with my clitoris, flicking it quickly with the side of my finger, so that I could come, too.

"He came. I felt him shoot inside me; then he took out his cock and shot more sperm over my bottom and down the back of my legs. I flicked my clitoris quicker and quicker, while David opened up my pussy and let his sperm slide out of me, all over my fingers, so that my clitoris was really slippery.

"I didn't even feel that orgasm coming. Usually I feel tense and rigid before I come, and I really have to strain for it. That time, it hit me over the head like a hammer, and all I can remember is shaking and trembling on the bed, my thighs squeezed tight together, saying 'Oh-oh-oh-oh-oh.'

"Our sex life never looked back after that day. I'm not saying it's always fantastic. It can't always be fantastic; otherwise we wouldn't appreciate the really fantastic moments when they happen. But these days they happen more and more often."

Susan concluded, "I don't behave like a whore. I don't behave like a downtrodden woman or the kept possession of a chauvinist pig. I am always myself, and whenever we make love, I always make sure that I enjoy myself. But what I failed to realize before was that David not only loved me, he thought that I was a turn-on. He's a man, as well as being my husband. Bare breasts give him a hard-on, *any* bare breasts; so I think it's up to me to make sure that the only bare breasts he's interested in are mine.

"I don't find it insulting or unfeminine to walk around the house on weekends with my breasts bare. I don't do it when I don't feel like it. Sometimes I walk around in nothing but a tanga; sometimes I walk around totally naked; sometimes I wear a skirt and a blouse and one of those bras that David calls my 'full armor.'

"I'm much more confident now in all kinds of ways. I'm much more sure of myself. And I don't mind telling David what I like in bed. Recently, for instance, if you'll excuse my blushes, I've had a particular liking for David pushing two or three fingers up my bottom while we're making love. I like his fingers right in, right up to the knuckles, and I like him to massage his cock through the thin skin in between my pussy and my bottom. Sometimes it hurts, but it's one of those really pleasurable pains, when you can't tell whether you love it or you hate it.

"These days, I'll do anything for David and he'll do anything for me. I mean *anything*. We seem to have lost all of our inhibitions, and we're not afraid to teach each other what we enjoy. The other night, for instance, I showed David just the way I like him to stroke my clitoris; he'd always rubbed it too hard before and then wondered why I never reached an orgasm.

"No, there's nothing degrading in doing your best to make your husband happy. How can there be? It's flattering for me to think that I'm his fantasy woman, and I don't feel degraded by being his centerfold pinup. These days we're closer than ever, I'm sexually satisfied, and I believe that David is, too."

Susan also remarked that her day-to-day friendship with her husband had improved as a result of their more communicative sex life and that they regularly talked more, discussed more news and topical items, went out together more, and generally felt like "a strong, better-balanced couple."

Their relationship had lost almost all of its inner frustrations.

Another interesting point emerged, and that was that once Susan had satisfied David's urge to see her walking bare-breasted around the house, he very rarely asked her to do it again—although she continued to do it from time to time whenever she felt like it, and he enjoyed it when she did. "There's something quietly erotic about sitting at the breakfast table half-naked, while the man who's sharing your breakfast is fully dressed. You know that Manet panting *Déjeuner sur l'herbe,* with all those men sitting fully dressed on the grass while the woman's sitting among them naked? It feels like that. You feel vulnerable, but attractive and very feminine."

Judging by the vast majority of cases that I have encountered, a wife who indulges her husband's secret sexual desires won't rid him of those desires. If oral sex turns him on, it will continue to turn him on. If rubber stockings turn him on, they will probably continue to do so for the rest of his natural days.

But she will find that his desires lose that obsessive tension that causes so much strain in sexual relationships. There is no desire that you think about more often than the desire that can never be fulfilled. As one husband told me, "I thought that I would never be able to ask Helen to go down on me.

She was one of those cool sophisticated beauties. I always thought that I was lucky to have married her. I couldn't see how I was ever going to ask her to take my penis into her mouth."

It is painfully noticeable that again and again, in cases of rape, the perpetrators forced their victims to have oral and anal sex: the two sexual acts that head the list of men's secret desires by far. In a large number of cases, the perpetrators were married, yet felt unable to ask their wives to satisfy these particular sexual cravings.

A convincingly high percentage of other women say that almost any man can be wooed away from his wife—not to mention his house and his children and even his career—by a woman who is prepared to open herself up to those sexual acts that his wife is unwilling to perform . . . or that he feels reluctant to ask her to perform.

This is Christine, thirty-three, from Philadelphia, Pennsylvania, who recently married a forty-one-year-old executive who had left his first wife and three children in order to set up home with her in Camden, New Jersey. "I honestly believe that Jerry truly loved his first wife, Carla, for most of their married life. In fact, in a way I think he still loves her now. But when I first met him at a promotional party, two years ago, we started talking, it was like opening floodgates. Within minutes we were talking as intimately as if we had known each other for years. Our attraction wasn't all sexual, by any means, and still isn't. But men do respond very quickly to assertive women, and I believe that part of what makes a woman assertive is her attitude toward sex.

"We had dinner together that first evening; then Jerry asked me if I wanted to come to his hotel room for a nightcap. I told him I never wore them.

"We were both very attracted to each other by then, and when we got to Jerry's room, we started kissing immediately. He undressed me and made love to me. He was very gentle and quiet and considerate. I enjoyed our lovemaking, but he didn't give me an orgasm. Well, maybe I was too tired, maybe I'd had too much alcohol. But it was obvious that he was used to making love—how can I explain it?—almost reverently, and he didn't say a word the whole time. He didn't kiss me much, either. It was just as if he was used to his sexual desires being tolerated rather than enjoyed.

"We both fell asleep almost at once. We'd had a long day. But around two o'clock in the morning I woke up, and Jerry was lying naked beside me, fast asleep. I did what I thought was natural. I kissed him, and then I ran my tongue all the way down his stomach and took his penis into my mouth.

"It was all soft and curled up, and I could get all of it into my mouth. I sucked at it gently, and it started to swell. Soon he was totally hard—and awake, too. He didn't touch me; he just lay there, really tense. I enjoy oral sex provided I'm not forced into it, provided I'm not expected to do it, and provided I can do it at my own speed. I know a lot of women think there's something not quite nice about oral sex, but when you're relaxed and you're feeling really affectionate toward a man, there's nothing more arousing than having your mouth filled up with a huge hard penis, and feeling his first slippery juices on your tongue. You know then that you're giving him something, that you're in charge, that you can control his feelings, make him feel good.

"Anyway, Jerry lay back for a while, and I licked him and sucked him. Then he took himself out of my mouth and rolled me over and started making love to me again. I wasn't complaining, but he made love in exactly the same quiet, restrained way that he had before. After a while I was going crazy. I said, 'Fuck me, for heaven's sake. I mean fuck me, harder. Fuck me like you mean it. Fuck me like you want to. Tell me how much you like me. Tell me how much I turn you on.'

"He started to make love to me harder. But he still didn't do it with much conviction. It was like he was afraid. I began to scratch his back with my fingernails to get him aroused. I asked him what it was like, having his cock sucked. 'Tell me what it felt like. Tell me how much it turned you on.'

"In the end, he managed to say that it was terrific. Well, that wasn't very romantic or exciting, but it was better than silence. 'Terrific,' he said, 'fantastic.'

"After we'd finished making love, we lay together in each other's arms and he told me that Carla had never kissed his penis, ever. Not that he hadn't wanted her to. He'd tried to suggest it again and again, in a roundabout way. He'd even been reduced to maneuvering himself in bed so that his penis was sticking out of his pajamas, close to her face. All she'd ever done was tuck it back in for him.

"He'd tried to give her oral sex himself, but she'd always twisted herself away or wriggled herself downward so that he couldn't reach her vagina. 'Make love to me properly,' that's what she always used to say to him.

"He said their sex life wasn't terrible, he couldn't really complain that Carla was frigid or unwilling or anything. It was just that she didn't seem to be interested in anything adventurous, and he was always afraid of upsetting her.

"Well, I finished off that first night for him by kneeling over his face and letting him kiss me and lick me as much as he wanted to. That was the first time he really let go. He went on and on, sliding his tongue up inside my vagina and licking at my clitoris, and I must have had five orgasms kneeling over him like that, beautiful rippling orgasms one after the other, and still he wouldn't stop.

"I knew then that he would leave Carla for me. I didn't encourage him in any other way, except to make love to him. In fact, I warned him again and again that it was going to be stressful and difficult and that it would probably cost him a fortune. I didn't ask him to leave her. But we had gotten on together like a house on fire right from the very moment we met, and we had both satisfied each other in bed, and I knew that he wouldn't be able to go back to Carla and all that polite respectful lovemaking."

What was Jerry's point of view? "It wasn't easy to break up my marriage. I felt desperately guilty and responsible about it when it happened, and to some extent I still do. I'll admit that—to begin with—the attraction I felt for Christine was principally sexual. She was prepared to do things that Carla would never have done, even if I had stayed with Carla for the rest of my life."

Did he know that for sure?

"My relationship with Carla was friendly, affectionate, but never completely intimate. She was an excellent homemaker, a terrific hostess, a perfect mother. But she wasn't a friend; she wasn't close to me and she didn't understand what made me what I was—and I don't think that she wanted to, either. The difference between living with Christine and living with Carla is like the difference between real life and a movie. With Carla, I was just acting out a role: 'Carla's Husband was played by Gerry.' "

Did he think that there was anything he could have done to improve his sexual relationship with Carla, and consequently to save his marriage?

"Maybe ... right at the very beginning of our marriage. But in those days I didn't have the confidence or the knowledge. I'd had quite a few girlfriends, and I'd lived with one girl for seven months before I met and married Carla. But telling your nervous new wife that you feel like having your cock sucked isn't as easy as it sounds. Carla was a nice girl from a nice family. She didn't even know about oral sex before I met her. Leastways, she said she didn't. And I wasn't exactly the right person to tell her.

"There was a whole lot wrong with our relationship that didn't have anything to do with sex. It was empty. You know, like a hollow shell. Looks perfect on the outside, nothing on the inside. But sex is important in a marriage, and when you find somebody you can have a terrific and unaffected and unembarrassed sex relationship with, like I found with Christine, then, what alternatives do you have?

"I said to myself, 'Jerry, when it comes down to the bottom line, are you going to spend the rest of your life on this earth faithful to Carla and sexually frustrated, or are you going to leave her and live with Christine?

"You can call me selfish and uncaring. You probably think that I should have tried harder to make my marriage work. But I didn't want to lose Christine, and that's the decision I made."

How did Carla feel?

"I was taken completely by surprise when Jerry said that he had found another woman, I still find it impossible to forgive him. He kept arguing that our sex life was unsatisfying. To be quite frank, I couldn't understand that at all. I had always been a loving wife to him. I never refused him sex. There was no question of 'headaches,' or 'I don't feel like it tonight.' Quite often I let him make love to me when I was very tired after a hard day with the children and I didn't feel like sex at all. I don't suppose he mentioned that there were several times when I wanted to make love and he didn't. But then he wouldn't say that, would he? Everything was always my fault.

"I'm not sure what this fuss about oral sex is. I do know about oral sex, of course I do. I would have done it if he had told me that he wanted me to. If I had known that it meant the difference between saving our marriage and ending it, of course I would have done."

But not with any enthusiasm?

"I don't know. I was never given the chance."

What about other sexual techniques?

"I don't know. If he had wanted me to dress up in sexy underwear or something like that, I wouldn't have minded. I can't tell you about anything else. Jerry never asked me for anything out of the ordinary. All of these arguments about how our sex life was lacking didn't come up until he met Christine. If he thought it was so bad, why didn't he tell me before?

"The truth is that he fell for another woman, and that, once he'd told me he loved her and that he was going to leave me, his pride wouldn't allow him to come back. I feel sorry for him, more than anything else. He'll soon get tired of her, the same way he got tired of me. He's like that. I feel sorry for her, too."

The case of Jerry, Christine, and Carla is a classic example of noncommunication in a marriage: a textbook profile of the sudden breakdown of a marriage that appears on the outside (and sometimes to one or both partners) to be perfect.

There were three principal reasons why Jerry didn't tell Carla before he met Christine that their sex life was lacking

First, he hadn't actually realized how seriously it was lacking until he had made love to Christine.

Second, he had never known how to explain to Carla his secret desires for oral sex and other variations without upsetting her.

Third, he had already resigned himself to a routine sexual relationship of straightforward intercourse and had simply lost the will to revitalize the sexual side of their marriage.

You can see that the breakdown of Jerry and Carla's marriage wasn't all her fault, by any means. Nor was it all Jerry's fault, either. Jerry failed to articulate his sexual needs. Carla failed to understand that, like most men, Jerry wanted a little more out of their sex life than regular missionary-position intercourse.

Jerry says he tried to suggest oral sex to Carla. Carla says she had no idea that he wanted it.

Sex, of course, wasn't everything. But Jerry had always felt that his marriage to Carla was lacking in closeness and spontaneity, and their sexual problems were largely to blame for what Jerry described as "this emptiness, this role-playing." Once Jerry had experienced Christine's relaxed and adventurous attitude toward lovemaking, the chances of Jerry and Carla getting back together again were almost nil.

Interestingly, Jerry says that he no longer feels a critical urge for oral sex, or any other sexual variation. "If I feel like it, I do it, and that takes all the frustration and the pressure out of it. Christine never says no to me. Likewise, I never say no to her. If I'm working on the car on the weekend and she comes out to the garage and says she wants to make love, then we make love. It's bliss. We never hide anything from each other, and I hope we never will."

Jerry's feelings are echoed by almost every other man whose wives or lovers have agreed to satisfy their secret sexual fantasies. "I used to have fantasies every night about Priscilla dressing up in stockings and a garter belt. The whole idea of it turned me on so strong that it made my head ring. Then, one day I plucked up the nerve to ask her to do it, and she did it. I came out of the shower, and she was lying on the bed wearing shiny black stockings and a frilly black garter belt and nothing else. And do you know something? After all of that frustration and all of that fantasy, it wasn't anything extraspecial. I enjoyed it. I'm not saying I didn't. She still dresses up like that sometimes, and that's great. But it's taken all the pressure out of it, you know? If you can't do something, you feel like it's important, you feel like it really matters. But when you can, well, then, it's normal and you take it for granted.

"There's one thing I learned, and that is that I love Priscilla for herself, and not for her stockings."

Priscilla obviously learned something, too: the power of positive sexual thinking. If you think sexy, you'll be sexy. And those other women had better look to their laurels.

Questionnaire:
What Do You Think He Secretly Desires?

Think carefully about your husband or lover and then ask yourself the following questions. If you don't know the answers to any of them, it's time you did. Your new sex life depends on knowing what he wants. Either ask him outright or give him a Xerox copy of the questionnaire at the end of Chapter 2.

1) He would like me to perform oral sex on him   YES/NO/DON'T KNOW
2) He would like me to wear sexy underwear in bed   YES/NO/DON'T KNOW
3) He would like us to watch erotic videos together   YES/NO/DON'T KNOW
4) He would like to perform oral sex on me   YES/NO/DON'T KNOW
5) He would like make love to me outdoors   YES/NO/DON'T KNOW
6) He would like to use a sex aid while making love (dildo, vibrating egg, clitoral stimulator, and so forth)   YES/NO/DON'T KNOW
7) He would like me to welcome him home in the nude   YES/NO/DON'T KNOW
8) He would like to tie me up while making love   YES/NO/DON'T KNOW
9) He would like to take erotic photographs of me   YES/NO/DON'T KNOW
10) He would like to watch me masturbate   YES/NO/DON'T KNOW
11) He would like me to masturbate him   YES/NO/DON'T KNOW
12) He would like me to take the initiative in bed more often   YES/NO/DON'T KNOW

13) He would like to have anal sex with
    me   YES/NO/DON'T KNOW
14) He would like to watch me urinate
    YES/NO/DON'T KNOW
15) He would like to make love more frequently
    YES/NO/DON'T KNOW
16) He would like me to bite him or scratch
    him or hurt him while we are making
    love   YES/NO/DON'T KNOW
17) He would like me to tie him up while
    making love   YES/NO/DON'T KNOW
18) He would like me to shave off my pubic hair
    YES/NO/DON'T KNOW
19) He would like me to talk dirty to him
    YES/NO/DON'T KNOW
20) He has a secret sexual desire which he
    thinks is too extreme to tell me about
    YES/NO/DON'T KNOW
21) Another woman could excite him in bed
    more than I can   YES/NO/DON'T KNOW

If you scored more than fifteen YESes, then your
man is fairly typical and you know your man fairly
well. Except for question 21, every question was taken
(not in order of preference) from a survey of men's
secret sexual desires. Even the most contented of
husbands expressed an interest in watching their
wives masturbate, or watching them go to the bathroom, or seeing their "bikini-areas" shaved. Men
have a much more visual response to sexual stimuli
than women, and these are all prime examples.

If you scored more than eight DON'T KNOWs, then
it's high time you gave your man the questionnaire
at the end of Chapter Two and checked his answers very carefully. You don't know him as well
as you ought to.

If you scored more than five NOs . . . you'd better
read on.

2

Make the Best of Your Body

As Betty Dodson discovered, a startlingly small percentage of women have a clear idea of what their sexual anatomy looks like and how it works, or how to make the very best of it during lovemaking. Many admit to feelings that there is something embarrassing or even shameful about their vaginas— even in this so-called liberated age when you can go to your friendly corner store and buy a magazine filled with color pictures of girls with their legs wide open.

Jean, a twenty-one-year-old secretary from Seattle, Washington, wrote me, "Whenever I am sexually aroused, my vagina becomes extremely wet, and I find this deeply embarrassing. Sometimes, when I have been kissing my fiancé, my panties are soaking. We have made love several times, but each time I have managed to go to the bathroom first and hide my panties and wipe myself with Kleenex. But what am I going to do when we are married?"

She didn't realize that, instead of being cursed, she was very lucky. If you produce a copious amount of vaginal lubricant before intercourse, it helps to makes sex much easier and much more exciting. It facilitates the insertion of your lover's penis into your vagina, and although it is practically odorless, it does have a taste and an aroma that men find highly stimulating.

Erotic literature, which is a very good way of discovering what turns men on, is teeming with

59

references to "sweet, damp loveholes," "juicy slits," and "drinking at her delicious fountain."

To most men, the wetness of a woman's vagina is proof of their own sexual attractiveness, and instead of being turned off, they respond very positively to damp panties. Jean should have flaunted them, not hidden them.

As I have suggested in my previous books, women should spend some time becoming acquainted with their own bodies. You do not have to attend a Betty Dodson–style consciousness-raising group, at which women used to display and touch and even taste one another's vaginas. But you can certainly get to know your body in the privacy of your own home. In fact, almost all sexual therapists agree that self-examination and self-caressing are very helpful factors in developing confidence, and in learning to make the best of your body.

This is Eleanor, a homemaker from Elizabeth, New Jersey, now twenty-eight, and very contentedly married.

"My mother was always very uptight about anything to do with sex. I never saw her undressed, and she always locked the bathroom door. I learned almost everything I knew about sex—which wasn't very much—from conversations with other girls in the school playground. If I hadn't, my first period would have taken me completely by surprise.

"My first marriage was a disaster. I was only nineteen, and a virgin, and I didn't know anything about lovemaking at all. The trouble is, neither did my husband. He would shove himself into me, push himself in and out until he came, and that would be the end of it.

"After two or three months of marriage, I began to get profoundly depressed, and in the end I had to have therapy. My first therapist was a man, and he didn't help me at all. In fact, in many ways he made things worse because he made me feel that somehow everything was my fault. Then, when he was on vacation, I talked to a woman therapist, and it was like a revelation, you know? She began to talk about my sexual relationship with my husband, and she asked me what it was like. I said, 'Fine, we have sex two or three times a week.' I'd already told that to the male therapist, and he'd said, 'Good, no problems there.'

"But the woman therapist asked me what our lovemaking was like. Was I satisfied? I said I supposed so. Did my husband give me orgasms? I said, 'What?' She said, did I have climaxes, orgasms? Well, of course, I didn't even know what climaxes were. She asked me if my husband ever caressed me sexually in any other way apart from straightforward intercourse. Did he ever stroke my clitoris, for example?

"Well, again, I didn't even know what my clitoris was.

"I was very embarrassed and ashamed at being so ignorant, but the therapist told me that I shouldn't be. It wasn't at all unusual for women to know almost nothing about sex, and just as little about their own bodies."

"She asked me if I had any objection to her showing me exactly what she was talking about. Of course I said no, not at all. I was desperate for anything that would help our sex life. So she lifted her dress and took off her panties, and sat on the chair in front of me with her legs apart, totally unashamed, and actually showed me where her clitoris was, where her urethra was, how her vaginal lips protected the opening.

"I was embarrassed at first, I have to admit, but she was so matter-of-fact and so interesting about sex that I quickly lost all of my embarrassment. She said that if I was going to improve my sex life I was going to have to take control of it myself. I was going to have to discover what turned me on, both physically and mentally, so that when we started to make love, I knew what I was trying to achieve in terms of arousal and satisfaction.

"She showed me the way in which she rubbed

her own clitoris during intercourse to make herself more excited. She showed me which sexual positions she preferred ... the ones in which her husband's penis gave her the most stimulation.

"She said that half the battle in improving your sex life is to learn how to be turned on yourself, because nothing turns a man on more than knowing that he has excited you—and nothing does more for his ego than knowing that he has satisfied you.

"It sounds crazy, doesn't it, but I never thought of going to bed with a man before with the specific intention of enjoying myself as much as possible."

Eleanor's therapist was quite right. Knowing your own body and being clear about your own sexual desires are an important part of the positive sexual attitude that will make you the kind of woman your man has always wanted. Eleanor's first marriage broke up before she was able to salvage it—but for other reasons apart from sex. Her husband was fired from his job for alcoholism and shortly afterward he started to hit her. She took her therapist's advice and quit while she was ahead.

But a large proportion of marriages that break up because of sexual difficulties do so because of the man's feeling that he is unable to satisfy his wife in bed—a feeling that he often rationalizes by accusing her of "frigidity."

Real "frigidity," however, is extremely rare, and even if your sex life is sparse and unsatisfying, the likelihood is that you are not suffering from it and never have done. And you can do something to make your man feel that you are sexier. Today, right now. And every day.

I have discussed the female sexual organs in detail in previous books—most recently in *More Ways to Drive Your Man Wild in Bed.* But for the purposes of improving your sex technique in a way that will reward you almost immediately with greater stimulaton and satisfaction, you should set aside a quiet hour this afternoon and experiment with self-arousal.

A great many women shy away from touching

themselves, although almost every woman has masturbated at one time or another, and some perfectly contented wives continue to masturbate throughout their married lives—not because they are sexually frustrated, but simply because they enjoy it.

What you will be doing, however, is learning more about yourself and what arouses you physically in order to improve your sex life with your husband or lover.

This self-discovery will be very much facilitated if you have a vibrator or a dildo or some large smooth phallic object that you can use to simulate your partner's penis. If not, you can use your fingers, but you may not be able to decide what sexual positions arouse you without the help of an object that can reproduce the penetration and the tugging of a penis.

Vibrators are freely available these days in drugstores, or mail-order through the small-ads sections of men's sex magazines. They are available in extraordinary variety, from tiny purse-sized vibrators called Lady Fingers to massive ten-inch vibrators with knobbly latex sleeves on them called Stallions. You can even buy plastic reproductions of a man's hand with a vibrating finger—called, believe it or not, a Clitboy. But for the purposes of exploring your own sexual responses, the best buy is either a simple rocket-shaped vibrator with a latex sleeve to simulate the shape of a real penis, or a boxed kit usually called a Female Pleasure Kit or Ladies' Joy Kit, or something similar. This offers a five-inch vibrator and a selection of different latex sleeves that can be used for clitoral, vaginal, or anal stimulation.

Beathe Bengtsson, a thirty-eight-year-old private sex therapist I met while working in Stockholm, in Sweden, advised women to choose a time for sexual self-stimulation when they knew that there was no risk of them being interrupted for at least two hours.

"It is vital that her mind should be completely empty of other considerations. She shouldn't be worrying, you see, about anybody calling, or what she is going to be cooking that evening, or whether her partner may come home unexpectedly. This is her time. It is important to her well-being and to her whole life. Therefore, she must allow herself to be selfish, and to indulge herself without any guilt or fear."

Beathe recommended that you should take a bath or a shower with a luxury soap or gel—preferably a new fragrance you haven't tried before—to heighten your sense of pampering yourself and to stimulate your sense of smell. You should also take time to paint your nails, pluck your eyebrows, depilate your legs—do all those little cosmetic chores that heighten your femininity and your sense of looking good.

Beathe is personally in favor of women trimming or shaving off their pubic hair. "Well, very many women do it anyway these days, because of the way that swimsuits are designed, but from a sexual point of view it has the advantage of displaying a woman's vulva much more clearly. Once a woman has removed her pubic hair, she can see that her vulva is not just a hidden slit behind a secret forest, but a beautiful shape in itself, a part of her body she can be proud to display.

"Apart from this, many men find that a shaved vulva is highly erotic. You must remember that men respond to sexual stimuli with their eyes, and to be able to see clearly their woman's vulva for the first time is usually a startling and very arousing experience for them.

"It does not have to be done all the time. Sometimes the hair can be allowed to grow back, if you wish. But I recommend it for this first session of self-stimulation because it will allow women to see their sexual parts very distinctly. Also, if they are in a strong mood for sex with their partners when they return home at the end of the day, the partner will be immediately stimulated by what he sees, and that will assist the loving."

As an extra add to relaxation, Beathe suggested

"a glass of wine, too, perhaps—but not too much. Your senses should be very alert, very responsive."

Once showered and groomed, you should find a comfortable well-lit place to sit or lie. A large arm-chair is often better than a bed, because you can sit with your legs supported by the arms, and your body raised so that you can see your vulva more easily. Make sure that you have everything around you that you need: your vibrator, if you are using one; your glass of wine; and of course your hand mirror so that you can examine yourself in detail. Beathe suggested that you should position yourself so that you can reflect sunlight or lamplight with your hand mirror to illuminate your vulva.

As you open your legs, your outer lips, your labia majora, will part to reveal your inner lips, your labia minora, and these will part to reveal your vestibule, into which your vagina and your urethra, or urine duct, both open.

Your clitoris is at the front of your vulva, where your inner lips join, about an inch and a half in front of your vagina. It is a small lump of tissue about the size of a pea.

The inner lips form a protective hood over the clitoris called a prepuce. In some women, the inner lips also join together behind the clitoris, to form a frenulum. Whether you have a frenulum or not, it makes no difference to your sexual responsiveness.

Actually, your whole clitoris is an organ about an inch long, but most of it is buried inside you. All you can see—even when you stretch your inner lips wide apart—is the tip of the clitoris, called the glans. You can feel the rest of it underneath the skin just above your glans.

Every woman's clitoris varies. Some have tiny glans that are barely visible; others have glans that are half an inch wide. The clitoris itself can vary, too. Some are short, some are long, some are fat, some are thin.

Your potential sexiness is not measured in any way by the size or the shape of your clitoris, any more than a man's potential sexiness is affected by the size or the shape of his penis. Some erotic stories talk about "her prominent clitoris" as if that somehow makes a woman sexier, and many men believe that a large clitoris is a sign of an especially responsive woman. Simply not true. There are several African tribes that encourage their girls to massage their labia and their clitorises from a very early age, in order to enlarge them, with the aim of increasing their enjoyment of sex. But women with small clitorises that are positioned so high up that they are practically invisible are just as capable of enjoying satisfying sex as their much more prominent sisters.

Your clitoris is similar in many ways to your lover's penis. When you were a tiny embryo in your mother's womb, before your sex could be determined, you had a lump of tissue between your legs that was indistinguishable from the lump of tissue between a boy embryo's legs. In a boy, however, this lump developed into a penis; in you, it grew into a clitoris.

Unlike the penis, of course, the clitoris has no opening in it. But, like the penis, it is made up of two rods of spongy tissue known as the corpora cavernosa. When you become sexually excited, these rods of tissue fill up with blood, just the way that the penis fills up with blood, and your clitoris becomes bigger, although it cannot become erect the way the penis does.

The corpora cavernosa go backward and sideways to connect up with the pelvic bones on either side of your vagina. They are covered by a pair of muscles that, when they tighten, prevent blood from escaping from the corpora cavernosa, so that the tissues remain engorged.

Connected to the underneath of the clitoris is another muscle called the bulbo-spongiosus (sexy names, aren't they?). This muscle is very similar to the muscle that rhythmically contracts when your partner has his climax and shoots out semen. When you have an orgasm, this muscle rhythmically contracts in a very similar way, and in its turn causes rhythmic contractions to the outer part of your vagina.

Your clitoris is crammed with nerve fibers that carry signals to your brain. These fibers join together with other fibers around the vagina to form a single nerve. Between the fibers are little structures called Pacinian corpuscles, which are highly sensitive to touch. There are corpuscles throughout your clitoris, but there is an especially dense crowd of them around the glans.

Some women have many more Pacinian corpuscles than others, and some researchers think this is the reason why clitoral sensitivity varies so much.

Although the penis and the clitoris are so similar, they respond completely differently to sexual stimulation, and this is why it is so important for you to understand how you are made and what happens to you when you become sexually excited. It's important for your partner to understand it, too, because far too many men believe that the way to stimulate a woman is to rub her clitoris as ferociously as they would rub their own penises.

To start with, your clitoris responds much more slowly than your partner's penis, whether it is being stimulated by intercourse or by self-arousal.

His penis will stiffen almost immediately when he is turned on. But you will already have started to secrete vaginal lubrication before your clitoris begins to swell ... and your clitoris will not swell by nearly such dramatic proportions as his penis.

It will, however, respond more quickly if it is stroked directly, rather than if stimulation is confined to your breasts or your vagina.

You can try timing your own responses by, first of all, caressing your breasts and your nipples, then by stroking and fingering your vagina, then by stroking your clitoris.

One of the greatest fallacies surrounding the clitoris is that direct contact between the clitoris and the man's body is necessary for full sexual pleasure and orgasm. Misguided lovers can even buy "clitoral stimulators," which encircle the base of the man's penis during lovemaking, with rubber protrusions that rub directly against the clitoris during intercourse.

But in most lovemaking positions, it is very difficult for your partner to keep up constant contact with the clitoris, and in some of them it is absolutely impossible. Not only that, when you reach the final phases of sexual excitement, just before orgasm, your clitoris actually withdraws beneath its hood, almost completely out of sight.

What stimulates you to orgasm during intercourse is the thrusting of your partner's erect penis in and out of your vagina, which tugs rhythmically on your whole vaginal area and stimulates your clitoris indirectly.

That is not to say that direct stroking of your clitoris can't make for exciting foreplay, or that it isn't a pleasurable and helpful adjunct to intercourse. But it is interesting to note that when women arouse themselves, only a small proportion use direct and systematic touching of their glans. Some actually find direct touching to be irritating and uncomfortable. Mostly, women prefer to stroke their labia minora, or to press rhythmically on the pubic mound just above their vulva. Some can bring themselves to orgasm simply by rhythmically squeezing their thighs together.

Again, techniques vary widely from individual to individual. Some women like to rub themselves quite hard, while a feather touch is quite enough for others.

Watching yourself closely in your hand mirror, you should arouse yourself by your preferred technique. As you become more and more sexually aroused, watch for any changes in the movements you use. Do you stroke yourself harder, quicker? Do you like to open your vulva wider, or do you prefer to squeeze your legs closer together? Do you like inserting your fingers into your vagina? Do you like tugging your vaginal lips outward?

It is only by watching yourself closely as you arouse yourself that you will learn how to respond more quickly to your partner, and how to guide him into turning you on more effectively.

As Beathe remarked, "One of the greatest causes of conflict and difficulty in sexual relationships is that men are far more readily aroused than women. Therefore it often happens even among mature and experienced lovers that the man will have finished, and feel quite satisfied, while the woman has only just started to feel excited. The frustration and the resentment that this disparity causes is tremendous, and every woman should make it her aim not only to make sure that her partner is satisfied, but that he knows how to satisfy her, too.

"It is not enough in this day and age for women to expect their husbands to be accomplished lovers, and to leave everything to them. Women should be experts, at least as far as their own responses are concerned."

Studying the way in which you arouse yourself can give you crucial information about how to get more out of your sex life. If you find that it usually takes you a long time to become aroused, then you should ensure that you indulge in plenty of foreplay before you actually have intercourse, so that by the time your partner penetrates you with his penis, you have already had at least one orgasm, or are close enough to be reasonably certain of reaching one during intercourse.

You cannot expect your partner to know intuitively how much stimulation you need before intercourse in order to be fairly sure of achieving satisfaction.

I am not pretending that it is an easy thing to tell the man in your life that you need more sexual satisfaction, particularly if he currently believes that he is the world's greatest lover, which 99 percent of men do. To begin with, you may be wiser not to, because what you want is a rejuvenated sex life, not a huge and unpleasant row about his wounded virility. Later, when things have started to improve, you can compliment him on being "better than ever before."

My feeling is that it is not at all dishonest to initiate new sexual excitements in your marriage simply by doing them, and showing your man just how much you enjoy them. When he sees how much more excited you are, then that will excite him, too, and you won't even have to encourage him anymore.

You will, however, have to say to yourself that you are going to throw off all your sexual inhibitions, that you are going to plunge headfirst into a new and stimulating sex life, and that if your partner shows an inclination for some particular sexual adventure, you are at least going to give it a try.

If you feel you need more stimulation before intercourse than he's been giving you, start playing with him more and teasing him more. When you go to bed, kiss him and caress him, and wriggle away if he shows any signs of heaving himself on top of you and performing yet another routine act of missionary-position sex.

Massage his penis between your breasts, kiss it and suck it, and guide him as subtly as you can into giving you the kind of stimulation you prefer.

If you can see by the way in which you stimulate yourself in the mirror that you have a distinct preference for long-sustained but very light stimulation before intercourese, then you could try coaxing your partner into caressing your clitoris with his tongue.

Here's Sandy, thirty-one, a dress-designer from Oakland, California. "I was never satisfied by sex, not through four years of marriage. I could never achieve a climax during lovemaking, never. For Dennis' sake I always had to pretend that I was climaxing, but after four years I was so frustrated and depressed that I started having all kinds of peculiar symptoms, like migraine headaches and sickness and all kinds of things.

"I could always have a climax by masturbating. But it took me a long time. I had to masturbate for maybe twenty minutes sometimes, even longer if I lost my concentration. I needed very light flicking on my clitoris, you know, so light that I could scarcely feel it; if it was any harder, it just put me off. I couldn't stand any distractions, either, like a television, or somebody walking around upstairs.

"In the end I was so low that I talked to a friend of mine about it, and I was amazed that she used to suffer almost the exact same problem. She was like me: she'd let it go on for so long that she was afraid to tell her husband about it in case she hurt his feelings. And what would he say to her? 'If you were so damned dissatisfied, why didn't you tell me before?' But the point is, you go on hoping it's going to work itself out, and you don't want to tell the man you love that he's not satisfying you, do you? I mean, sex is important for women, but for men it's like proof that they're men.

"If I'd have told Jimmy that I'd been faking orgasms ever since we were married, I think he would have walked straight out the door and never come back.

"My friend said she'd read some novel that was mainly trashy, but it had a bit in it about a woman who had trained her cat to lick her cunt. I mean, the idea was pretty far-out, you know how scratchy cat's tongues are, but the idea of having her cunt licked really turned her on. So that night she encouraged her husband to do it. She did it by going down on *him* first of all, even though she'd never liked oral sex too much. Then she simply sat on top of him in the sixty-nine position with her open cunt right in front of his face, and I guess she couldn't have given him much more obvious encouragement than that.

"I did exactly the selfsame thing with Jimmy. When we went to bed that night and we were watching television, I started fondling him and rubbing him with my hand, until he went hard; then I drew back the sheets and took him into my mouth.

"I was frightened, terrified, for all kinds of reasons. I was frightened in case he didn't like it. I was frightened in case he thought something was wrong. I was frightened he was going to realize that he hadn't been satisfying me. I was frightened in case he thought I'd been to bed with some other man.

"But I kept on licking him and sucking him, really slowly, because I wanted to set a really slow pace to our lovemaking, and I ran my tongue all the way down his cock and took his balls into my mouth one by one, and then I rolled his cock all around my face and kissed it and really made a meal out of it. I glanced at him once or twice, and he was watching me with his faraway look in his eyes and I realized how much I was turning him on. And when I realized how much I was turning him on, I was turned on, too.

"That was the secret that I guess I hadn't realized in all of those four years of marriage: that lovemaking isn't something that men do to women. Lovemaking is something that you do between you. You don't get anything out of it unless you put something into it, and sometimes you have to put something into it that you don't think you're going to like too much, like sucking your husband's cock. But if you don't do anything like that for him, how can you expect him to do anything like that for you?

"I did what my friend had done and sat astride Dennis' chest, and I didn't have to say a word. He took hold of the cheeks of my bottom in his hands and opened them up wide, and he slid his tongue right inside my cunt. I really shivered. It was such an incredible feeling I wasn't sure whether I liked it or not. But then his tongue circled around and around my cunt, and he started to flick with the tip of his tongue right at the tip of my clitoris, so light and delicate that I could scarcely feel it. I think I fell in love with him all over again, and he must have been able to tell how much he was turning me on, because he kept on licking light and quick, and I kept on thinking of that cat licking that woman in the story, and I was more excited than I'd ever been.

"I held his cock straight up in my hand and ran my tongue around and around the rim of it, and kissed it, and then pushed it deep into my cheek and sucked at it. Not only was Dennis turning me on, but I was turning myself on, too.

"Dennis still doesn't know it—or if he does, he hasn't said anything—but that night he gave me my first orgasm. I can't even remember what hit me. One minute he was licking and licking, and the next I was all bunched up tight and shaking like an earthquake, and my cunt was in this incredible spasm that felt so good that I couldn't stand it. It felt as if it went on forever.

"The incredible thing was that the television had been playing all this time, really loud, and I hadn't even noticed it.

"Dennis made love to me after that. It didn't last very long, he was too excited, but then it didn't have to. When he came, I had another orgasm, just a small one, like an aftershock. Ripples, you know? Delicious ripples.

"It isn't always as good as that. Sometimes it's fantastic and sometimes it's just, you know, nice. But after that night I never had to pretend any longer. And Dennis goes down on me and licks me without my necessarily having to do the same to him. I think we've agreed that we're reasonably sexually compatible these days. At least our marriage has a chance, which is more than it had before."

By studying your own preferences in sexual stimulation, you could—like Sandy—find a way of altering your partner's lovemaking so that he turns you on more effectively and satisfies you more often. Sandy found that after she had been lightly stimulated by her husband's tongue or finger, her preferred position for intercourse if she hadn't already reached a climax was to lie with her back to her husband and her legs drawn up. Thus, while he was making love to her, she could press her thighs together and exert gentle and rhythmical pressure on her clitoris, which would almost always bring her to orgasm.

If she had reached a climax, then she considered that "almost any position will do," although she did have a liking for sitting on top of her husband. "When I do that, his cock goes very deep inside me, and I can have dozens of those little ripples when he touches the neck of my womb."

Using your vibrator, without switching on the motor, you can try out the comparative sensations of different lovemaking positions. Push the vibrator in and out of your vagina and notice at the same time how it tugs—in just the same way as your partner's penis tugs—at your vaginal lips, and thus indirectly stimulates your clitoris.

Women show a distinct preference for lovemaking from the rear, in that position known as "spoons," and from the side, in which they sit on their lover's lap.

"When men are on top of you, you feel overwhelmed, and often they don't appreciate just how much they weigh. Sometimes I like it, because I want to be overwhelmed, I want to be dominated. But it doesn't allow you to do much except what an Indian boyfriend of mine called 'straightforward jig-a-jig.' There's no room for much subtlety, if you know what I mean."

From the rear, however, your lover can reach around to caress your breasts and stomach. He can also reach between your thighs and stimulate your clitoris. If he makes love to you from the side, he can stroke your clitoris and your anus at the same time, and also massage your vaginal lips while you are making love. Since he is not trying to support his own weight on his elbows at the same time, he is able to arouse you in these positions with a precise touch and a considerable degree of finesse.

I have never been an advocate of those mind-boggling illustrated books of "250 Different Sex Positions." They are for voyeurs, not for doers. Only four or five sexual positions are actually practical—by practical, I mean that they are more stimulating than strenuous—and to my mind the location, the mood, and the erotic rapport between lovers are far more important than twisting themselves up like Harry Houdini on his day off.

Once you have decided what kind of touch and stimulation arouses you the most, you can begin to work on how you can change the pattern of your sex life so that you get the very best out of it. For many women, who have no particular sexual difficulty except that their partners are usually too quick for them, it is often enough to introduce more foreplay into their lovemaking and then to make sure that they make love in the position they prefer.

You can do this the same way that Sandy did, by initiating lovemaking rather than waiting for your partner to make the first move. By doing that, you have a better chance of controlling the pace of your arousal and of making sure that your partner stimulates you in the way that turns you on the most: finger, tongue, or penis. Also, if you have already put yourself in a sexy frame of mind, before you start stimulating your partner, you are going to be considerably more aroused than usual when he eventually penetrates you, and closer to the possibility of being satisfied.

Sitting in your chair, watching your vulva closely in your mirror, you should try to simulate the sensations of intercourse with your vibrator. See how your lips swell and redden and how the glans of your clitoris enlarges. See how much lubricating fluid you produce. Feel—as only you can feel—the angles of thrust that excite you the most.

Some women particularly prefer to be penetrated from the rear because of the small extra amount of indirect rhythmic pressure that their lover's penis transmits to their clitoris. One twenty-six-year-old wife told me, "I like it from the side. My husband churns himself around in me, as if he were mixing molasses with a baseball bat." It didn't sound very romantic, but she assured me that it was "out of this world."

See if you can bring yourself to orgasm using the vibrator alone. You might not be able to manage it the first time you try, but if you caress yourself beforehand in your favorite way and then use the vibrator in the way that you would like your partner to use his penis, you should be able to achieve it sooner or later. It will help you to fine-tune your physical feelings so that you learn precisely what arouses you most effectively.

Some women find that their lovemaking is improved if they make a deliberate point of thinking about it all day, and physically working themselves up to it.

Nadine, a thirty-two-year-old insurance executive from New York City, told me how she fought another woman for the affections of her thirty-six-year-old husband, Thomas—and won.

"We'd been married for less than three years when one of my friends called me up and asked if I knew about Thomas and Lucy. I didn't know anything about Thomas and Lucy, except that Lucy was Thomas' secretary and that he was always saying how efficient and helpful she was.

"My first reaction was to have a real knockdown drag-out fight with Thomas. You two-timing bastard, all that kind of thing. But then I sat down and asked myself, Why? I thought we were happy. Why should he start carrying on with his secretary?

"I knew the answer even before I'd finished asking myself the question. It was S-E-X—or rather the distinct lack of S-E-X. I was always highly motivated, highly career-oriented. I worked hard and I worked long hours, and I guess I literally forgot about being a wife. We had a maid to clean the apartment, and both of us used to eat out practically every day, as part of our jobs. When I came home in the evening, I used to bring a whole lot of paperwork with me, and I rarely got to bed before one o'clock in the morning. Thomas used to try to make love to me, but I was always too tired. We used to go for weeks without making love, and then we did it only on Sunday mornings, before Thomas got up and made us some breakfast.

"Sex wasn't that exciting, either. Thomas would kiss me and then he would get on top of me, and we would move up and down, and that was it. I could never get into it, you know? I was always thinking about something else. I still loved him, but physically we weren't making any kind of contact at all. Sex was just a kind of relief. A token gesture to show that we were still married.

"But we weren't man and wife. We weren't even lovers. We just happened to share the same apartment. Now Thomas was going to bed with his secretary, and it was mostly my fault.

"So I made some decisions. I decided not to confront him with it. But I also decided I wanted us to stay married. That meant that I was going to have to fight for him, and the battleground was bed. I made up my mind that we were going to make love every night, if we possibly could. I was going to wear him out. If he still wanted to go out with Lucy after that, well, that would be the end of it. But I wasn't going to surrender my husband to some secretary without a fight.

"I spent hours thinking about sex. Like, what did I want out of it, and what did I think Thomas wanted out of it? Thomas was always very civilized, almost gentle, yet I had always felt that he had a slightly sadistic streak in him. He had rented the video of 9½ *Weeks* twice over. The second time he said he hadn't realized he had seen it before, but I ask you, Who can see 9½ *Weeks* and not realize they've seen it? So he watched it again.

"He had a couple of books in his den, too. An

illustrated version of *The Story of O,* and some Dutch book with drawings of girls making love in the open air.

"I borrowed *The Story of O* after he had left for work, and I took it to the office with me. I went to the ladies' bathroom around eleven o'clock that morning, and I undressed completely, and I sat on the toilet seat stark-naked and looked through this book, and stroked myself.

"I thought about Thomas making love to Lucy. I thought about Thomas making love to me. I got off the toilet and crouched on the floor, with my face pressed against the tiles. I had the fingers of my left hand right up inside me, and I was furiously stroking my clitoris with my right hand. There were pictures in *The Story of O* of fully dressed men casually inspecting naked women. That really excited me. I could imagine that I was one of those naked women and that I had to lie back obediently and open my legs so that they could look at me.

"Then somebody knocked on the toilet door and I had to stop, and quickly get myself dressed. I don't know what my staff would have thought if they had seen their elegant vice-president stark-naked on the floor of the executive toilets, furiously stroking herself."

But had she discovered anything about her sexual responses, both physical and mental?

"I took lunch by myself that day, brown-bagged it in my office with the door closed, thinking. I never would have considered myself the kind of woman who responds to a man being dominant. If anybody had ever asked me, I would have said, Well, I'm the dominant partner. But the fact is that I was longing for Thomas to take control of me, to tell me what to do, to be sexually strong with me. Thomas, for his part, was obviously feeling that I wasn't very interested in sex, and he didn't have the motivation to be strong.

"I didn't do anything that night, I was still unsure of myself. But the following morning I went around to Thomas' office on West Twenty-ninth Street, no appointment. He was in a meeting, but I told Lucy that it was urgent and could he come out for a while. I tried not to look at Lucy too much, but I couldn't help checking her out. She was brunette, like me, quite pretty, not so thin and not so tall.

"Thomas came out looking worried. I told him there was nothing wrong, but could he find us a private room where we wouldn't be disturbed. He took me along to a small office and then asked me again what I was doing there. So I showed him. I was wearing a button-through dress, and I unbuttoned it. Underneath I was wearing a black waspy basque and stockings tied with ribbons, and that was all. I said I needed him. I said I'd do anything. I turned around and placed my hands flat against the wall and opened up my legs and said, Fuck me.

"For one moment I thought he was going to refuse. I thought he was going to turn around and go straight back to his meeting and that was going to be the end of our marriage. But then I heard the key turning in the door, and he came up behind me and opened his pants and pushed himself straight into me.

"I was already turned on. I'd been mentally hyped up all morning, and when I had gone to the toilet at work and changed into the basque, I had masturbated myself until I was right on the edge of having a climax. Thomas was very strong, almost brutal. He gripped the top of my basque and wrenched it down while he was fucking me, so that he bared my breasts. He shoved himself into me again and again, and I had to bite my lip to stop myself from crying out. I had a climax and went totally weak at the knees, but he pulled me up again and kept on pushing himself into me.

"When he climaxed himself, he pulled himself out of me and shot sperm all over my back and my bottom and the backs of my thighs. I felt it sliding down my stockings. Then he turned me around and he kissed me like he hadn't kissed me since the day we were married.

"I didn't hold out any tremendous hopes that one sexual act was going to make all the difference to our marriage. But I was determined to change, if he wanted to stay, just like he had to change, too.

"He came back from work that evening at about six-thirty and I was waiting for him, all dressed up. He said, 'I'm glad you're dressed. We're going out to dinner tonight.' I said, 'What time did you reserve the table?' He said, 'Eight.' I said, 'That's good. I've got a present for you.'

"He didn't know what I meant until I lifted my dress. Instead of panties, I'd tied a red silk ribbon tightly around my waist, and in between my legs, so that it cut really deep into my vagina. Then I'd tied it in a big bow.

"We both learned to appreciate each other after that. I don't know what happened to Lucy because he never mentioned her again, although I think she still works there. You work so hard at everything else—at building your career, at making your home, at being healthy and successful and all the rest of it—sometimes it's easy to forget you have to work at sex, too.

"I mean—nice work, but still work."

I found it interesting that Nadine and Thomas had such neatly interlocking sexual needs: she had a taste for being (mildly) dominated, while he had a taste for being (mildly) dominant. Yet until their relationship was in danger of complete collapse, neither of them had explored the erotic possibilities that their sexual compatibility offered them.

Usually, a couple's secret sexual urges are less clearly defined, and less exotic. But the rewards for exploring them can be just as great, if not greater. And they are worth exploring as soon as possible—tonight, if you have the time. While Nadine was managing to save her marriage, she was a heartbeat away from losing her husband forever.

So, first define what you want out of your sexual

relationship—what physical fulfillment and how you think that you can achieve it. Then pluck up your courage, and go get it.

Questionnaire

Offer your partner this questionnaire to answer ... and see for yourself how well he understands your sexual needs.

1) My partner is completely satisfied with my lovemaking   YES/NO/DON'T KNOW
2) I do not spend enough time making her feel romantic before I start making love to her   YES/NO/DON'T KNOW
3) I know without fail how to stimulate my partner to orgasm   YES/NO/DON'T KNOW
4) I always make my partner feel that I appreciate the way she looks   YES/NO/DON'T KNOW
5) Somtimes I leave my partner feeling frustrated   YES/NO/DON'T KNOW
6) If she isn't satisfied after lovemaking, then it is usually her own fault   YES/NO/DON'T KNOW
7) I have an accurate knowledge of a woman's sexual organs   YES/NO/DON'T KNOW
8) I would know for sure if my partner were faking an orgasm   YES/NO/DON'T KNOW
9) I can exactly locate my partner's clitoris   YES/NO/NOT SURE
10) It is essential for a woman to have her clitoris stimulated to achieve a sexual climax   YES/NO/DON'T KNOW
11) My partner likes me stimulating her sexually with my tongue   YES/NO/DON'T KNOW

12) My partner has shown me the way she prefers to be aroused YES/NO/DON'T KNOW

13) My partner would like me to spend more time stimulating her before intercourse YES/NO/DON'T KNOW

14) Women with prominent clitorises are more easily aroused YES/NO/DON'T KNOW

15) Some sexual intercourse positions stimulate my partner more than others YES/NO/DON'T KNOW

16) Women prefer men to make love to them in the traditional man-on-top position YES/NO/DON'T KNOW

17) I have sexual urges that I have not told my partner about YES/NO/DON'T KNOW

18) My partner would be shocked if I told her some of my sexual fantasies YES/NO/DON'T KNOW

19) My partner does not mind if she has a sexual climax or not YES/NO/DON'T KNOW

20) Sometimes I feel frustrated with my partner because I cannot suggest certain sexual acts I would like to perform, in case she becomes angry or disgusted YES/NO/DON'T KNOW

Well, when he's answered, use your own knowledge and judgment to mark his sexual shrewdness!

3

The Sweet Touch of Success

"I slept with three boyfriends before I slept with my first husband, but I had no idea what a man actually looked like, naked. Not in any detail, not close up. A man's penis was something you felt, rather than saw. I would have been far too embarrassed to look at it, as if I was really interested in it."

This was Heidi, a twenty-nine-year-old phys-ed teacher from Minneapolis. Her blond hair, her figure, and her exceptional looks won her a prosperous husband ten years her senior, a man who showered her with gifts and compliments when they first dated but who was unfaithful to her only four months after they were married.

When she discovered that he was cheating, she confronted him with it and asked him why. "I loved him. I would have done everything."

But his reply was, "You might have tried to do everything you wanted. But you simply didn't know how."

Heidi was left confused, baffled, and miserable. After eighteen months she sued for divorce, and her action was uncontested, although her husband told her during the course of a long and acrimonious telephone call that she was "frigid" and "clumsy" and "sexually naïve."

In fact, Heidi's general sex education was reasonably good, compared with other women of her own age. She knew where babies came from, she knew about orgasm, she knew what a man's sex organs looked like—diagrammatically, from her school biology books; artistically, from postcards of Michelangelo's *David,* and photographically from copies of the now-defunct *Viva* magazine.

She had been involved in two or three "heavy-petting" relationships before the age of sixteen, when she lost her virginity. "I had allowed boys to touch my breasts and to touch me intimately with their fingers. I wasn't shy about sex. My mother had always been quite open about it and answered all of my questions about periods and birth control and stuff like that."

So, how had she failed so badly to please her husband?

"There were all kinds of reasons, and they weren't all sexual, although he tended to roll them all up into one easy reason: that I was useless in bed.

"Looking back on my marriage, I know now that I shouldn't have married him, because we simply weren't compatible. But I guess if our sex life had been good, we could have learned to get along.

"The trouble was, I simply didn't know how to arouse him or touch him or anything. When you're in biology class at school, they show you what the male sexual organs look like, but they sure don't prepare you for how to touch them. How's a girl supposed to know how hard she can grip a man's penis? Or how to stroke it so that he won't feel frustrated? It's like a man's testicles. You keep hearing terrible stories about how sensitive they are. I was afraid to look at them, almost, in case I gave him a hernia.

"If he had really cared about me, he would have tried to show me what he wanted, rather than trying to get it from another girl. But then I think a whole lot of men are like that. They have this particular sexual need, and if you don't know what it is, then they're sure not going to tell you. You're supposed to know.

"What I didn't understand until a whole lot later

was that he was probably too embarrassed to tell me. Too shy. And a little bit too macho, too. Like 'Why should I have to ask my woman to touch my cock?' My husband was the kind of man who wouldn't ask anybody for anything. He wouldn't even ask directions when he was lost, in case I thought that he didn't have total recall of every page of Rand-McNally. You think women are shy and ignorant about sex? I think men are three times shyer and three times more ignorant, and on top of that they're too proud to tell their wives what they want."

There's considerable truth in what Heidi said. Although men have easier access to sexual information—through the *Playboy Adviser,* for example, and magazines like *Penthouse Forum*—they often find it more difficult to ask for information and assistance on personal sexual matters, for fear of being thought to be less than virile.

Men are also much more frightened of taking the sexual initiative than you would think. That is why some of them come on absurdly macho, and others don't come on at all.

Wives who are accused of being "frigid"—and who have even come to believe that they are frigid—are very often not suffering from frigidity at all, but from their husband's ignorance and lack of basic sexual skills and refusal to ask for help.

So, quite often, it's up to you to provide that help, even though it hasn't been asked for. It's up to you to initiate more exciting sex. It's up to you to make sure that you're sexually satisfied.

One wife who tried Frederick's of Hollywood underwear to turn on her husband said, "The very worst thing that can happen is that you can have a good time."

It is those women who can show men what to do in bed—who can guide them and inform them and arouse them and make them feel good, and at the same time keep their sense of virility intact—it is those women who can take husbands away from wives, or who can keep their own husbands faithful.

A word on virility. "Virility" has become something of a pejorative term these days, so perhaps it's more accurate to talk instead about a man's sense of being a man.

In a loving sexual relationship, a feeling of virility has nothing to do with bullying or machismo or male domination. It is simply the masculine equivalent of your own sense of being a woman. When he's making love to you, your man needs a feeling of strength, a feeling of being able to please you and satisfy you, a feeling of being a hunter and a protector, and also, and very importantly, a feeling of being sexually attractive to you.

It is startling how many wives, once they have settled into the routine of marriage, forget to show their husbands that they still find them sexually attractive. Either they forget or else they no longer consider it necessary. "I thought I had him for life. I didn't think that I had to keep telling him how much he turned me on. I wouldn't have continued to stay with him if he hadn't turned me on, would I?"

So, if you want your man to feel better about you, make sure that you show him regularly and often just how you feel about him.

Time and time again I have found that the sexually demonstrative woman is the woman who attracts —and keeps—her men.

Let's go back to Heidi, who was accused by her husband of being naïve and frigid. Heidi said, "I always wanted to show him that I loved him. But the truth was that I didn't actually know how. When were in bed together, I didn't know what to do: how to hold him, how to turn him on. I was always afraid that I would touch him the wrong way and either hurt him or make him think that I was useless."

Although Heidi's husband was principally to blame for the breakup of their marriage, the chances were that she could have saved it, if she had wanted to, if she had been more sexually expert. As we have seen, you can't always rely on men to know what they're doing in bed. In fact, you can't *often* rely on men to know what they're doing in bed.

I questioned a cross section of men about what they considered to be the sexual shortcomings of their wives or girlfriends. Their answers were far more revealing of *their* shortcomings than those of their partners. They showed convincingly that, for all of their expectations, men frequently lack the confidence and the expertise to be good lovers. Therefore, they are frequently prey to women who can give them the confidence they lack and make them feel that they are attractive and accomplished lovers.

Over 67 percent of the men I questioned complained that their partners "never made the first move in bed." Over 64 percent complained that their partners "never touch or fondle my sex organs." Over 58 percent said that their partners "just lie there and expect me to do all the work."

And a whopping 73 percent protested that their partners "never touch me sexually except when we're in bed."

When I questioned the men's partners, a clear picture of the other side of the coin began to emerge. Over 61 percent of women said they wouldn't know how to make the first move in bed; 72 percent said they didn't usually touch their partner's sex organs because they weren't sure what to do; 52 percent said they wouldn't touch their partner's sex organs because they simply hadn't thought that their partners might like it. And 64 percent said they believed that "the man should take the lead in bed."

As for touching their partners when they were anywhere else except for the bedroom, a clear majority of women had never considered it, and when they did consider it, they didn't appear to think very much of the idea. "I don't know, it just doesn't seem right somehow for a woman to be putting her hand down a man's pants. It puts her in a position of making the first move." Of course it does. And that's *precisely* why men enjoy it. It is an unequivocal demonstration that he turns his woman on, and that she wants to have sex with him.

When it comes to men and sex, you can't be too unsubtle.

Here's Rhonda, who came home unexpectedly one day to catch sight of her fifty-four-year-old mother masturbating her fifty-six-year-old father while he calmly watched the San Diego Padres on TV.

"I walked in and there they were, on the couch. I was shocked. I turned around and walked straight out again. It wasn't so much that my parents were having sex. I knew they still made love. It wasn't their age, either. They're both fit and healthy and young for their age. It was the fact that my father was sitting there with his cock sticking out and my mother was sitting right next to him massaging it. I didn't even know that women did things like that.

"Anyway, my mother came up to my room later and talked to me. She said she was sorry, she hadn't expected me home so soon. I think she understood what was bothering me. She said that all men liked to be touched and fondled, the same way that women do. She said that if more women touched their husbands spontaneously, opened up their pants and just rubbed them and caressed them, then a whole lot more husbands would feel a whole lot happier.

"She said there was nothing dirty or juvenile about it. It was something that she liked to do and that my father really enjoyed."

Wise words from Rhonda's mother. Because Rhonda's mother understood that men have a very quick response to sexual stimuli, and while a woman may expect to be wooed and flattered and kissed before she begins to grow sexually aroused, a man can grow instantaneously erect if a woman starts opening up his pants and playing with his penis, even if she's a complete stranger.

A man can be stimulated into full and instantaneous erection by looking at a photograph of a woman whom he will never meet and can never hope to meet, and he can use that photograph as a stimulus to masturbate himself to complete climax within a matter of minutes, if not seconds.

It is very important for you to understand the immediacy of male sexual response, and also the powerful involuntary urge involved. While your sexual relationship with the man in your life should involve deep and emotional and communicative acts of lovemaking, you should also indulge him with playful acts of what the massage parlors call "relief."

- They help to break any sexual tension between you.
- They show him that you want him physically, and that he turns you on.
- They show that you're loving and selfless and that (with him, anyway) you're certainly not shy.
- Apart from that, they can be very exciting for both of you.

You will need the confidence to open up your man's pants and take hold of his erection and massage it just the right way. That was the confidence that Heidi lacked, that millions of women lack. "I'm afraid I'll do it wrong. I'm afraid he'll think that I'm useless and clumsy."

It is on the practical aspects of making love that almost all sex education falls down. There is no point at all in showing you diagrams of a man's penis and explaining how it works, and then saying, "That's it, get on with it. Make him come." For the same reason, I disapprove of sex books that show you scores of extraordinary positions in which to have intercourse—except, of course, for their value as an erotic stimulus. You might just as well publish a series of photographs of a man sitting in different positions in the driving seat of an Oldsmobile and call it "How to Drive a Car."

You do need to know how a man's sexual organs

work. Understanding what occurs inside will help you to understand what goes on outside. There is a chapter in *More Ways to Drive Your Man Wild in Bed* called "His Proudest Possession" that explains the inside intricacies of your partner's sexual equipment. But for the purposes of giving him the most exciting relief possible, all I'm going to describe here is how to manipulate your man to arouse him the most.

First of all, you have to choose your moment for doing it. Watching TV—(as Rhonda's parents were) —is always a good time. Your partner will already be relaxed and passive, and because it is so distracting, the flickering tube will help to take any undue intensity out of the proceedings. This is an act of simple sexual pleasure, that's all, a few minutes' play, and it does not necessarily have to lead to intercourse.

When two people live together, there are plenty of occasions when one of them will feel horny while the other doesn't. Or when they both feel mildly affectionate and sexy, but don't actually feel like intercourse. There is so much emphasis these days on "full and fulfilling lovemaking" that sexual play seems almost to have been forgotten. Yet sexual play is the area in which you can get to know your lover's tastes the best, and learn to give him the kind of sexual fulfillment that will really last out the years.

You should never be shy to touch your man's sexual organs at any time. To begin with, you may find he reacts with shyness or embarrassment or even shock. The secret is not to make your approach too much of a surprise. Men automatically double up to protect their sexual organs whenever they are touched without warning, and they experience an unpleasant sense of nervous reaction, quite apart from the silliness they are going to feel when they realize that they were doubling up to save themselves from nothing more threatening than you.

So do it gently and obviously. You can kiss him,

perhaps, while he's standing in the kitchen waiting for the coffee to perk, and slide your hand into his pants pocket. Then you can rhythmically squeeze and fondle his penis through his shorts, until you feel him begin to stiffen, which shouldn't take too long.

He may react adversely at first to your touching him sexually. This is because you are making a blatantly erotic advance without prior warning—which he doesn't expect his wife to do, remember. He may also feel at a disadvantage because you are making the running and you are obviously more turned on than he is. Some men display a surprisingly negative reaction to women whose sexual feelings are plainly more aroused than their own.

Keep your hands inside his pants pocket while you reach around with your other hand and open his zipper. This will make sure that your advance is not interrupted and that it does not become gauche and awkward. Smoothness and seductiveness and continuity are always essential in love play, especially in the early stages of arousal.

You can be as silly as you like, of course. You can kiss his cheeks and nibble his ears and call him your little flopsy-wopsy. But you should keep your grip on the shaft of his penis through his pants pocket with one hand, while you open up his shorts (or tug them down, if he's wearing bikini-shorts) and expose the glans of his penis with the other.

Pull his penis as far out of his fly as it will come. You don't have to be particularly gentle with it. A hardened penis can take a reasonable amount of robust handling. Peel back the foreskin—if he has one—and then grip his penis so that the ball of your thumb is resting just below the ridge of his glans, the tip of your forefinger is touching the vertical web of delicate skin just below the opening of his penis (known as the frenulum), and your remaining fingers rest naturally down the underside of the shaft.

Then rub his penis with a slow but persistent

rhythm, tugging the thinner skin of his shaft downward with each stroke. While you do so, you can tickle and tease the more sensitive frenulum with your forefinger and occasionally circle the tip of your finger around the opening of his glans.

As he becomes more aroused, he will begin to secrete clear slippery lubricating fluid from the tip of his penis, and you can use this fluid to lubricate your forefinger as you caress the underside of his shaft.

As he becomes more aroused, you can rub his penis harder and faster, and you can move your thumb upward slightly, so that it is resting against the glans. At this stage, you can grip his penis as hard as you like, as long as you make sure that you don't dig your fingernails into it.

Remember that the nerve endings that arouse him are all concentrated around the glans and the upper part of the shaft, just below the ridge. Many women make the mistake of rubbing a man's penis too far down the shaft, where there are far fewer sensitive nerve endings, and the result is that they succeed in doing nothing but causing their lovers a strong feeling of frustration. It is just as bad as if he fingered you in the wrong place.

While you rub him quickly with your right hand, reach inside his shorts with your left hand and lift his balls out of his pants. Make sure you do this very carefully so that you don't cause him any discomfort. Cup his balls with your left hand, caressing them and *gently* squeezing them, and use your middle finger to stroke him in between his balls. If you press your middle finger upward, in between his balls, you will be able to feel the hardened shaft of his penis through the skin of his scrotal sac. Place your finger on this spot and stimulate him with a persistent tugging motion, rather as if you were trying to erase a smudge from a sheet of clean paper.

As he approaches ejaculation, you will feel his balls tighten, and the preejaculatory fluid will flow more copiously. Keep rubbing with the same quick, firm movements, and don't stop when the first spurt of sperm shoots out. After the second spurt, stop rubbing and slowly squeeze his penis, tugging the skin of the shaft downward from the glans to increase his pleasure. Very gently rotate your index finger around the opening of his glans, using his sperm as a lubricant, while his erection begins to subside.

You should remember that immediately after his climax, your partner will be sensitive to any further robust handling. If you continue to rub his penis as hard as you were before, he will find the sensation quite irritating. But you should try to do a little more than zip him up and give him a cheery pat on the fly. A few moments of gentle caressing is not only pleasant, but finishes the love game off with lingering affection.

This is Georgina, a thirty-six-year-old twice-married receptionist. "I learned from my second husband, Jack, just how much men like you to fondle them sexually. They really like it, and yet the extraordinary thing is that women just don't do it. You can put your hand into a man's pants at any time of the day, and he'll adore it. You don't need any preliminaries, you don't need to *say* anything even. I did it once to him after a dinner party, when he was calling our friends on the telephone to make sure they'd managed to drive home okay. I don't know why I did it particularly. I'd been drinking champagne and I was a little tipsy. But while he was talking, I just opened up his pants and started to stroke him.

"He adored it. Long after the other people had hung up, he stood in the kitchen with his eyes tight shut, gripping the phone, while I stroked him and stroked him. He shot sperm all over. I never saw so much of it before. I asked him later whether he had liked it, and he said, 'Liked it?' As far as he was concerned, it was fantastic.

"I do it pretty often now, just when I happen to

feel like it. So many women don't understand how quickly a man can get turned on. Jack was working up a ladder the other day, painting the ceiling in the kitchen, and I stood underneath the ladder and opened up his overalls and took out his cock. I kissed it and stroked it, and it only took him about a minute to come.

"It's had an effect on our sex life, for sure. We make love much more often. Nine out of ten times, if I start stroking him like that, we'll wind up making love wherever we happen to be. He was out washing the car about two weeks ago, and I came out and talked to him for a while, then I came up behind him and slipped my hands into the pockets of his jeans. I squeezed his cock and opened up his jeans and pulled it out. I held it tight and rubbed it up against the side of the car, which was all wet and soapy. He turned around and kissed me. He fondled my breasts through my T-shirt, and of course his hands were all wet, so it was just like a wet-T-shirt contest. My nipples were hard and sticking out, and he gripped them with his teeth, right through the cotton of my T-shirt, gently but really sexily. While he was doing that, he lifted up my skirt and pulled down my panties. He bent down and took them right off me. Then he picked me up and sat me on the wet hood of the car. He opened up my legs, and he stood right up against the car and pushed his cock into me. We were making love so frantically that the car was bouncing up and down. I couldn't reach an orgasm like that, I was too uncomfortable, but then Jack picked me up and laid me down on the grass, and we finished making love like that.

"I know it all sounds like a fantasy, but it actually happened. He and I had never made love like that before, never, it was absolutely fantastic. After it was all over, he went into the house to fetch a bottle of wine, and I lay on the grass with my skirt up around my waist and my T-shirt soaking wet, and I looked up at the sky, and believe me, I felt good."

Many wives told me that it had simply never occurred to them to touch their husbands sexually at any other time apart from bedtime or occasionally bathtime. Quite a large proportion never touched their husbands sexually at all—"not unless he touches me first." The idea of taking the initiative in lovemaking, even when they were in bed, seemed quite foreign to them.

But this is David, a thirty-one-year-old electrical engineer from Miami, Florida: "I married Jean, my high-school sweetheart. It was never a bad marriage, I can't badmouth Jean for anything. But both of us were pretty ignorant when it came to sex. We knew enough to kiss and cuddle and to produce two children, but when I used to read *Playboy*, there was all this stuff about people having incredible sex lives and doing all kinds of far-out things, and I always used to feel that Jean wasn't too interested in sex. I mean, she didn't seem to object when I wanted to make love, but she never dressed sexy or did anything sexy. I bought her some really sexy underwear once. I mean, I went through sheer hell walking into the store and buying it, I was so darned embarrassed. But I couldn't pluck up enough courage to give it to her. In the end I put it into the trash.

"Then I met Margot. It was completely by accident, I wasn't out looking for anybody else. Margot was the sister of a high-school friend of mine. I met him for a a drink, and Margot came along, too. She was small, dark, terrific figure. Very vivacious, very talkative. She was wearing this tight white dress that had every guy in the street turning around with his eyeballs out on stalks. She and I got along pretty well, but at the beginning there was no question of my thinking that I was going to have an affair with her, or anything like that.

"About two weeks later I saw Margot downtown with a girlfriend of hers. We started to talk and I invited them both for a quick drink. The girlfriend had one drink and had to go, so that left Margot and me together. She asked me if I wanted to come to a party at the weekend. I told her I was married. She said she couldn't believe it, I was far too young. Anyway she said if I changed my mind I was still welcome.

"I thought about it all week, and after a whole lot of soul-searching I decided to go. I thought, Hell, I *am* young, why shouldn't I? I guess at that moment I was deciding to be unfaithful, or at least giving myself the opportunity to be unfaithful.

"I told Jean I had to go to Fort Lauderdale to talk to some guy about an electrical contract. It wasn't unusual for me to have to do estimating work at weekends. So I went to the party. It was great. I felt like I was sixteen again. Margot and me started dancing together and then we started kissing and we went to bed together.

"It was exciting to go to bed with a different girl, but it wasn't all that different. I felt real guilty about it afterward. But on Monday, Margot called around to my office. She looked really terrific in these tight jeans and this checkered blouse. She asked what I was doing for lunch and I told her I didn't have time for lunch, I had too much work. Anyway, I was standing by the filing cabinet looking through some papers when she came up and stood beside me, and started stroking the front of my slacks. I asked her what she was doing, and she said, 'Well, since you don't have time for lunch, this'll do.'

"She took out my cock and she started to rub it up and down. She really knew how to make you feel good. Somebody was out in the corridor so we stood behind the door and she kept on rubbing and rubbing and kissing me and running her hand through my hair.

"She was rubbing me so quick that after only a couple of minutes I was ready to come. I said, 'I'm coming,' so she said, 'Here,' and she opened up the zipper of her jeans, and when I started coming, she held her jeans open so that all of my jism squirted inside her jeans. Then she zipped them up again, kissed me, and left. I've got to tell you, I was left standing in the office like a man struck by lightning.

"I couldn't think about anything else but Margot for the rest of the day. Let's put it this way: if a girl walks into your office, gives you the very best hand job you've ever had in your life, and then spends the rest of the day walking around with her jeans filled up with your jism, it's not the kind of thing that you instantly forget, is it?

"The trouble was, I really felt like I'd let Jean down. I still loved her, and I wasn't prepared to risk losing her, not for Margot, not for anybody, and I sure didn't want to lose my kids. So I actually thought to myself, If Margot can do things like that, why can't Jean?

"A couple of nights later when I was lying in bed and it was hot and I was feeling horny, I took hold of Jean's hand and I put it on my cock. She was silent for a long time and she tried to take it away, but I kept on holding it there. She said, 'What do you want me to do?' And so I said to her, 'This cock is yours as well as mine, you can touch and you can squeeze it whenever you want to.' So, very slow and cautious, she started to rub it. I said, 'You can do it harder than that, and quicker, too.' So she did. And when it was really stiff, she got on top of me and made love to me. *She* made love to *me*, and it was great.

"We had a long talk about sex. It wasn't particularly easy. But I suddenly realized that Jean enjoyed it just as much as I did, and she'd been thinking that I wasn't interested. I said, 'You're crazy, I'm just like every other man in the world, I think about nothing but sex all day.'

"Things have been a whole lot better since then. We're still learning. We've bought ourselves a couple of books and four or five sexy videos, but Jean isn't crazy about the videos because they have too many lesbian scenes. But these days she doesn't mind if I come up behind her when she's washing the dishes and slip my hand inside of her panties, and when I'm working some evenings, she'll come into the spare room naked and sit on my knee and open up my pants and see if she can work me up.

"She always succeeds.

"Occasionally I think about Margot walking around Miami with her jeans wet, but that wasn't for me, you know? Not so long as Jean can act so sexy."

You shouldn't feel reticent about touching your man sexually just because you're not sure that you're going to stimulate him properly. If you can put yourself into a positive frame of mind so that you want to touch him and want to fondle him, then willingness is all you need. You'll soon learn what kind of stimulation he prefers, particularly if you ask him—and asking him doesn't take too much courage. All you have to do, as you massage his penis, is murmur, "Is this good? How about this?"

But there are some special ways of manipulating your man that will give him extra pleasure.

• *The Pump*   Grasp his penis tightly in your clenched fist, just below the ridge of the glans, with the ball of your thumb pressed against the opening. Then masturbate him with a strong pumping action, occasionally flexing your thumb so that you press hard against the opening. When he ejaculates, keep your thumb pressed tight against the opening to intensify the pressure of his climax.

• *The Cobra*   Hold the underside of his penis in the palm of your hand, so that the heel of your hand is lightly pressing against his testicles, the shaft is gently pressed between thumb and pinkie, and your middle finger is touching him just below the opening of his glans. Stroke him up and down, using your thumb and your pinkie to tug down on the sensitive skin just below the ridge of the glans, and the tips of your index and third fingers to titillate the rim on either side of his frenulum. As he approaches climax, move your hand up the shaft of his penis so that you can grip it more firmly and give him the more robust stimulation for which he will now be feeling the need.

• *The Twist*   Grip his erect penis so that the ball of your thumb is just below the opening of the glans, and your index finger is hooked just beneath the ridge on the upper side. Rub his penis up and down, but as you do so, twist your wrist around so that you are pulling at the looser skin of the shaft and actually twisting the glans so that opening is facing away from you. You will discover how hard you can twist it by trial and error. You will hear *Ouch* when you are twisting too hard. As he ejaculates, squeeze and twist as the same time.

• *The Birdcage*   This is a teasing and particularly effective way to stimulate your man's penis when you have very long fingernails. Cup your hand over the top of his glans and grip him lightly all around the upper shaft, with the ball of your thumb against his frenulum. Rub him very lightly and very quickly, making sure that the upper side of his glans constantly rubs against the palm of your hand. The Birdcage technique takes longer, and if your hand is growing tired, you may prefer to change your grip to a straightforward pump action toward the end. But if you can manage to keep up the speed and the lightness of the Birdcage until he ejaculates, he will be rewarded with a particularly jolting climax, and you will be rewarded with a tremendous spurt of semen up your wrist.

• *Shanghai Special*   This is a two-handed technique, easier to manage when your lover is naked, but highly arousing, with a climax of very high intensity guaranteed. Lie beside him—on his right, if you are right-handed; on his left, if you are a southpaw. Grasp his penis as comfortably as you can, just below the glans. Give him very short, hard, throbbing rubs, squeezing his penis tightly each time you rub. Keep your rubbing as quick as you can consistently manage. With your other hand, coax him into slightly raising the leg that is nearer to you, and then slip your hand beneath it and cup and caress his testicles, running the tip of your finger down the central dividing line of his scrotum, until you reach the sensitive raised area between his testicles and his anus, which is called the perineum. When he begins to secret preejaculatory lubricant, stop rubbing him for a moment, moisten your index finger (or moisten it, alternatively, with lubricant from your vagina, which is more copious, more effective, and for him, much more stimulating). Lavish as much lubricant as you can around his anus and then insert your left-hand index finger as deeply as you can into his ass. Up to the knuckle, if you can. Go back to your short, rhythmic rubbing, and as you do so, stimulate him anally with a smooth, repetitive, beckoning gesture with your index finger. As you feel a climax approaching, increase the speed of the rubbing and increase the depth and strength of your anal stimulation. You can even try inserting two fingers into his ass, or three. When he ejaculates, smear his semen all the way down the shaft of his penis and between his legs.

• *Hard Sell*   Grip the base of his penis just above his testicles as tightly as you can with your left hand, so that his penis becomes extra-engorged with blood, and extremely hard. At the same time pull down the loose skin of the shaft and keep it pulled down, under constant pressure. Lubricate your right hand with a copious amount of KY or similar jelly, and masturbate his hard, strained penis quickly and lightly until he ejaculates.

It won't take you long to discover your lover's favorite techniques. You'll be able to judge what he likes the most by how quickly and how explosively he comes. But every man has different sexual responses and different sexual tastes, and if you find that he comes more quickly when you masturbate him one particular way, and if you find that he enjoys his climax more demonstratively when you masturbate him in another particular way, you can custom your stimulation to suit his needs—either by selecting particular techniques from those described here or by mix-and-matching them with techniques of your own.

You may find, for example, that he prefers the Birdcage grip for starters, followed by the Shanghai Special technique. You may find that he likes a smooth, scarcely touching massage to begin with, followed by the vigorous stimulation of the Pump.

Edna, a twenty-three-year-old secretary from Toledo, Ohio, described to me a "pastry-rolling" technique that always turned her husband on: massaging his penis in the palms of her hands while flicking his glans with the ball of her thumb. When he ejaculted, she stretched apart the opening of his glans with both of her thumbs—simply because she enjoyed watching the sperm spurting out of him.

As Linda Lovelace once wrote, "It's great to see a cock doing its thing so close to your face—when that beautiful thing aims at you and shoots. Wow! Instant glory!"

Other masturbatory variations I have been told about include rubbing your lover's penis with Vicks or mentholated shaving cream, which gives an interesting tingle; pressing a handful of crushed ice against his testicles as he climaxes; and cat's-cradling his testicles with rubber bands while you massage his shaft.

You could try out these techniques one day if you've a mind to. But in my opinion they lack the spontaneity that makes the touching of your partner's genitals so exciting. What counts most is freshness and surprise.

Lilian's story sums up the sweet touch of success.

She was nineteen years old when she married Kevin, an auto mechanic from Omaha, Nebraska. In her own words, she knew "sweet nothing" about sex. Their relationship, which started off passionately, quickly degenerated into confusion and frustration.

"Kevin made love to me pretty regularly, three or four times a week, sometimes more, but somehow it didn't seem like it was going anyplace. We just did the same thing every time, and that was it. Watch television, maybe drink a little wine, make love, kiss good night, and that was it, every time. I thought to myself, Hey, am I still going to be drinking a little wine, kissing, and making love, you know, when I'm forty years old? The same thing, three times a week, forever?

"What I didn't understand was that Kevin felt pretty much the same way, but he didn't know any more about sex than I did. His dad had once told him to give a woman a little wine, and sweet-talk her, and kiss her, and then you could make love to her, and that's precisely what he did, time after time, no variation. But he was just as frustrated as I was.

"One day I met a friend of mine from high school. She was married, too. She persuaded me to come to a cocktail lounge with her. We had a couple of drinks and started talking about all kinds of things: men, babies, mothers-in-law, sex.

"I suppose I must have had one too many whiskey sours, because I told her that I thought there was something wrong with me sexually. I told her that I loved Kevin, but that our lovemaking wasn't particularly exciting. I don't know, sex just didn't seem to have any life in it.

"Anyway, my friend said that if I felt that way about it, I ought to tell Kevin just how I felt. I told her that he would go crazy, if I did. He was real sensitive about everything, you know, like his car, and his hairstyle, and the way he danced; and if he caught another guy looking at me, he'd go ape. And if I told him I wasn't satisfied in bed, God, he'd probably sulk for about a half a century.

"But anyway my friend said you don't have to tell him you're bored. Just get him going. Of course, I didn't have the first idea how. But my friend said, 'Come on to him just as soon as he gets home, or when he's watching TV—anytime.'

"She said the whole thing was not to be shy. 'He's your husband, after all,' that's what she said, 'the guy you live with. If you can't be open and natural with him, then who can you be open and natural with?'

"I was determined that as soon as Kevin stepped into the apartment that evening that I was going to drag him into the bedroom and make mad passionate love to him. But he came home real tired and somehow I didn't have the nerve. I thought, Well, after supper maybe. But he had to work on a whole lot of accounts after supper. I took a bath and sprayed myself with perfume, and I put on one of his shirts. He always liked me wearing his shirts: he said it made me look like a little innocent girl.

"Well, I waited and waited till about eleven o'clock and he was still working, so in the end I went through to the living room and he was sitting at the dining table with his spectacles on and his calculator and all the books.

"He said, 'It's okay, honey, I'll be coming to bed in a minute.' But I told him I'd wait, and I sat down on the floor next to him, resting my head on his leg. You're not going to believe this, but I was frightened. But I remembered what my friend had said. 'He's your husband, after all.' So I reached in between his legs and started stroking his cock through his pants. Real gentle, just like stroking a cat.

"He took off his spectacles and looked at me and smiled and said, 'Heyyy, I'm trying to get some work done here.' But I said, 'Don't mind me.' And he put his spectacles back on and carried on working. It seemed like it was okay to touch him like that, just so long as he was concentrating on something else, like he wasn't at all responsible for what was happening.

"After a while his cock began to grow real hard, so I tugged open his zipper and eased it out. He kept on working, didn't look at me, but I told him, 'This is beautiful,' and slowly massaged his cock up and down until it was fully hard. I thought to myself, I love this man, and I love his cock. I massaged him real slow, because I wanted this to last forever. I suddenly understood how fantastic it was to be married and to be able to touch a man's cock whenever you felt like it.

"I massaged him quicker, and then I moved around so that I was kneeling right between his legs. I licked the whole length of his cock with my tongue. I'd never done that before, I'd never kissed his cock or anything like that. But now I felt like I was in charge, do you understand what I'm saying? It wasn't him seducing me; it was me seducing him, and I could do anything I wanted.

"I kept on massaging him with one hand and unbuttoned my shirt with my other hand. Then I knelt right up and kissed him. He was so turned on that his eyes were tight shut and he could scarcely kiss me back.

"I felt him coming. I actually felt his cock swell up in my hand and go into spasm. Then he was shooting out sperm all over my breasts. I kissed him and bit his tongue, and then I massaged that sperm all over my breasts like it was moisturizing cream. I couldn't believe that I was doing anything so—well, you know, so sexual. There was sperm dripping from my nipples. I felt as if I had managed to free myself, somehow, get rid of all of my inhibitions about sex.

"I wasn't frightened of it anymore. I thought, Here's a man shooting his sperm all over me, and it's exciting, and it's not going to hurt me. In fact, it did the opposite. The dam broke, as far as our sex lives were concerned. We started making love whenever we felt like it and however we felt like it. There isn't a single sexual thing I wouldn't do with Kevin. He's my husband."

Questionnaire

This questionnaire is designed to give you a picture of how far you would be prepared to go to introduce spontaneous stimulation into your sex life. Be truthful!

1) I think bedtime is the only right time for sex   AGREE/DISAGREE
2) There is nothing wrong with touching your partner sexually at any time   AGREE/DISAGREE
3) I would consider taking my clothes off to excite my partner at any time of the day   AGREE/DISAGREE
4) If I feel like having sex, I do not wait for my partner to make the first move   AGREE/DISAGREE
5) A woman should make her sexual demands clear to her partner   AGREE/DISAGREE
6) I do not like the idea of touching my partner sexually   AGREE/DISAGREE
7) Anything other than straightforward intercourse is perverted   AGREE/DISAGREE
8) I am frightened by the idea of sexual variations   AGREE/DISAGREE
9) It would excite me to masturbate my partner   AGREE/DISAGREE
10) Women who take the sexual initiative are making themselves cheap   AGREE/DISAGREE
11) I would consider any sexual act with my partner   AGREE/DISAGREE
12) I would like to be better at sex   AGREE/DISAGREE

13) It is my partner's responsibility to make our sex life varied and interesting   AGREE/DISAGREE

14) There are certain private acts that I would never do in front of my partner AGREE/DISAGREE

15) I like the idea of my partner climaxing on different parts of my body   AGREE/DISAGREE

16) I enjoy satisfying my partner sexually even when I do not feel like sex myself AGREE/DISAGREE

If you AGREED with six or more of the following questions, then you are a sexually creative woman who should have no trouble at all in improving your sex life; 2, 3, 4, 5, 9, 11, 15, 16.

If you AGREED with six or more of the following questions, then you should think to yourself, Isn't it time I contributed more to our sexual relationship? 1, 6, 7, 8, 10, 12, 13, 14.

4

What Men Want . . . And How to Give It to Them

As we saw earlier, men can be sexually aroused much more quickly than women, and by erotic stimuli that have nothing to do with their current sexual relationship. Your man can love you till it hurts, but that still doesn't make him impervious to photographs of naked girls whose names he doesn't even know, or by fantasies that, if you recounted them in the cold light of day, would sound depraved beyond all reason.

Women who understand this side of a man's sexual personality, and who realize that his erotic daydreaming is not just harmless, but can be used as a positive stimulus in their sexual relationships, are the women who catch and keep the men they want.

As far as the man in your life is concerned, you ought to be one of them . . . unless you want him to fall prey to some woman who is—and can, and does!

Here's Stephanie, a twenty-six-year-old saleswoman in a well-known Manhattan department store: "I first met Mike when he came into the store to buy some perfume for his wife. Working on the perfume counter is a tremendous place for picking up married men. They're always considerate; otherwise, they wouldn't be there, buying perfume for their wives in the first place. They're usually wealthy—well, you know what perfume costs! And they're usually a little bit helpless, because they don't quite know what they ought to be buying.

"You couldn't dream of a better combination. Especially when you add those husbands who have had an argument with their wives and are buying perfume to make it up to them. Usually they're still just a little bit resentful against their wives, and if you're really clever, you can exploit that to your own advantage.

"I expect you think I sound terrible. The cold, calculating husband-stealer. But married men are almost always the most attractive and the nicest, and if their wives can't satisfy them, why should I worry? Besides, Mike was the only husband I actually stole for keeps. All the others went back to their wives."

Mike was a thirty-six-year-old attorney who had come into the store where Stephanie worked to buy a birthday gift for his Laura, his wife of eight years' standing. Stephanie found him "incredibly attractive, but very reserved and pent-up when it came to talking to women, like a lot of married men are. You know, they've forgotten how to deal with attractive girls."

Stephanie was certainly attractive. Very petite (five feet, three inches) with blond curls and an eyecatching figure. She had studied drama and dance after graduating from high school and had a very bright, outgoing personality.

She helped Mike make his choice of perfume, and he left, apparently satisfied. Three days later, however, he was back at the store, to ask Stephanie out to dinner. His wife had gone to Buffalo to visit her parents; he had a free weekend.

"He took me to dinner and he poured out his heart. How much he cared for Laura, but didn't love her. How guilty she made him feel. They had a six-year-old son, Carl, and Mike felt guilty about him, too. And Laura kept nagging him for another child, but in all conscience he couldn't think of having another one. You have children with people you love, right? Not just to shut somebody up.

"Mike wasn't seriously messed up, but he was

married to the wrong woman, that was all. He wanted a woman who was sexier, who wasn't so prissy. More of a friend than a homemaker. I'll always remember, we were walking back to my apartment on East Forty-ninth, arm in arm, and he said, 'I wanted a woman like Fannie Fox, and what did I get? Fannie Farmer!' Then he laughed, and said, 'Wrong damn Fannie!'

"We went back to my apartment and he made love to me. He was gorgeous. There is no man on earth who can make love to you like a married man who's frustrated with his wife. Strong, caring, powerful . . . mmmmffff! You get everything he's learned and everything he'd like to do, all rolled into one.

"In the morning, I felt this incredible feeling between my legs, and I opened my eyes, and he was licking my pussy. Ohhh, I tell you, I just lay back and let him do it to me. He kept sliding his tongue all the way down my slit, all the way to my asshole, and then he'd flick it up again and give me this light teasing play right on my clitoris, so light, just like butterfly's wings.

"And he really relished it, you know? He practically bathed his face in my pussy juice. I reached down with both of my hands and I stretched open my pussy lips for him, as wide as I could, because he loved it so much, and if it turned him on, it turned me on, too.

"He pushed his tongue right inside my pussy, licking around and around, and then he brought it up a little way and pushed the tip of it into my pee hole, too, and no man had ever done that to me before. He really knew how to turn me on. I didn't think I was going to have a climax, but it crept up on me and hit me right over the back of the head; and the next thing I knew I was jerking up and down on the bed like somebody had jolted me with fifty million volts.

"He didn't take his mouth away, even then. He was sucking the juice out of my pussy even while I was actually coming. And then he closed his whole mouth over my clitoris and teased me with the tip of his tongue, so light that he was scarcely touching me, but it kept giving me these aftershocks, one after the other. It drove me crazy! In fact, it got so I couldn't stand it and I had to tell him to stop.

"It was then that he got up on top of me and made love to me. Beautifully slow . . . and when he came, I could feel every single drop of it inside me. He lay there afterward and we shared a cigarette and he told me that I was fantastic. He said that Laura would never let him go down on her. She always turned over or pushed his head away. She didn't like the idea of him doing it. She said it was degrading for a man to do that to a woman. I said, 'How can it be degrading if you love her?' But he said that it was one of those things he hadn't pressed her about, you know, because it wouldn't have gotten him anywhere.

"Then he told me that pretty early on in their marriage, he'd thrown his pajamas in the laundry basket and seen a pair of her panties lying there. He'd lifted them out, and they'd been stained. You know, a little pee perhaps, and just normal vaginal juice. White lacy panties, that's what he said. And he'd pressed them against his face, just to smell her pussy smell. And of course she'd walked right into the bathroom and caught him doing it and thought he was some kind of freak.

"She wouldn't even let him touch her afterward, not for weeks.

"He said that whole incident had almost finished their marriage right then and there. She was so totally straight. I mean, she was sexually intolerant to the point where she didn't even like him to fuck her from behind. But all he wanted to do was to show her that he loved her, every bit of her, even the *smell* of her."

Mike's enthusiasm for the taste and smell of a woman's body was not even slightly unusual. A very few men are not particularly keen on women's vaginal secretions, but most of them find the sexual lubricants that women produce to be highly stimulating. Throughout the ages, erotic literature has been crammed with delirious references to women's juices, and the delight that men take in drinking them.

"Sophie was all of a tremble," ran a story in the Victorian erotic magazine *The Pearl*. "She wriggled herself most excitedly over my mouth, and I licked up her virgin spendings as they came down in a thick creamy emission."

It's true, however, that many women feel hesitant about allowing their partners to stimulate them orally.

Jenny Fabian, authoress of *Groupie* and probably the most renowned fellatrice of the 1960s, once told me that she hated the idea of a man's face between her legs.

And Naomi, a twenty-four-year-old homemaker from Minneapolis, Minnesota, said, "I'd always been brought up to think that a woman's vagina was unclean. I couldn't believe it when Michael wanted to kiss me there. I just didn't know how to react."

But most men have a powerful urge to kiss their partners' vulva, even if they find it difficult to say so, and equally difficult to put into practice.

It is critical that you shouldn't rebuff any attempt by the man in your life to stimulate you with his mouth—whether you're shy about it, or whether you simply "don't like the idea." If you put him off, you won't only be missing out on one of the most intimate and stimulating sexual things that a man can do for a woman. You'll be denting your partner's confidence in his attractiveness, in his sexual technique, and in his belief that you really love him.

For most men, licking a woman's vulva is a demonstration of their sexual devotion, just as sucking a man's penis, for most women, is a demonstration of their sexual devotion.

If you rebuff that devotion, even once, it's going to be doubly difficult for your man to be aroused in the same spontaneous way the next time around. He may be aching to lick your vagina. But the possibility of being told no is always going to stay his tongue. He's always going to be thinking, Will she let me do it? If she does let me do it, will she really enjoy it? Or will she just be suffering it because she thinks she ought to?

This is another "other woman"—Kate, twenty-eight, from Sherman Oaks, California: "I always enjoyed oral sex. When you kiss your lover's penis or he kisses your cunt, it's one of those times one of you can do something for the other, really intimately, really showing them how much you care. It's like a statement. You say to him, I want your penis in my mouth and your sperm down my throat. Or he's saying to you, I want to put my tongue inside your cunt and suck all your juices.

"A man can make love to you in all kinds of different ways, but when he kisses your cunt, to me, that's commitment, that's passion, and that turns me on. But it's one of those things that really turns men on, too, especially if you show them how much you want them to do it. I always encourage my lovers to do it. Well, I say always—I haven't had that many, only six. But sometimes I'll sit with my feet up on the couch in the afternoon wearing my short Japanese bathrobe, reading a book, and when my lover-of-the-moment comes in, he'll sit at the end of the couch, and I'll loosen my robe and say, 'Kiss me.'

"And I can tell you, ten out of ten times, he will, and I've never had anything but sheer pleasure out of it yet.

"It doesn't sound like much of a technique, does it? But women just don't seem to offer themselves to men like that, even though men go wild for it. Men go crazy for it. Believe me, if I were writing a book for women, to tell them how to keep their husbands happy, I'd say, show them your cunt as often as you can, because men simply love looking at your cunt. They'll never admit it, but they do.

When he wakes up next to you in the morning, pretend to be lying asleep on your back with your legs wide apart. You can keep your eyes closed, but let him have a good long uninterrupted look at your cunt. Let him finger it if he wants to, pretend you're still asleep. Cunts are a mystery to most men, they're dying to see what they're like. Make sure you walk around the house in a baby-doll nightdress, without any panties on, and that you bend over at every possible opportunity.

"Sit on top of your husband when he's lying in bed, sit on his chest, sit on his face. You've got a beautiful cunt, that's what I'd say, what are you hiding it for?

"The very worst thing that's going to happen to you is that you're going to get very turned on.

"I always shave my pubic hair and use hair remover. That's another thing that men like, although you won't get many of them to admit it. It makes your cunt nicer for them to kiss, too, without any hair. I started to shave when swimsuits began to get really cut high on the thigh, and when I saw what it did to my sex life, I kept on doing it."

From pratical experience with six lovers, Kate found out that if she thought positive sexual thoughts and encouraged her lovers to do what they secretly wanted to do, her love life was almost always satisfying and exciting.

I asked her how many of those six lovers—all married—had been happy with their wives.

"Four out of six. Those four liked their wives. They loved their wives. But somehow they felt they couldn't ask them to do what they wanted. One of my lovers was the handsomest guy that ever lived; you couldn't imagine any woman telling him no. But one night, when I was a little drunk, I guided his cock up my ass, for a change, just because I felt like it, and do you know something? He went crazy. He fucked me up my ass like a tornado. He fucked me four times up my ass that night. I was sore, but I couldn't stop him. I didn't want to stop him. When I went to the bathroom the next morning, my ass was red like a rose, and sperm poured out of it like you wouldn't believe. His wife had never allowed him to do that—not even once."

Of course, the crucial question is, If my husband's secret sexual desires are secret, how do I find out what they are?

How can I satisfy his hidden urges if he won't tell me that he's got them?

Well, the answer is this. You identify your husband's secret sexual urges in the same way that a laboratory identifies an allergy. You try just about everything until you hit the jackpot.

With sex, you won't have to try too many possibilities before you strike lucky. And, believe me, if you put yourself into an amenable frame of mind, you'll enjoy trying.

Stephanie conclusively won Mike's affection by wearing a white lacy pair of panties for three days without washing them—"even after we'd made love the night before." She pulled them up tight between her legs whenever she wore them to make sure that she stained them as much as possible, then she wrapped them up in pretty tissue paper and slipped them into Mike's briefcase.

"He found this surprise package when he was looking for his calculator. He opened it up and found a tiny pair of dirty panties. He told me later that he folded them up in his hand and sat at his desk the whole afternoon, smelling the smell of our lovemaking and the smell of my body; and he said that was absolute heaven."

Many women express strong reservations about male sexual urges. They feel threatened and degraded by them. In every expression of a male sexual urge in which a woman has been hurt or humiliated or made to take part in a sexual act she didn't positively encourage and enjoy, I would agree.

A recent survey for the British women's magazine *Options* showed that 95 percent of women were opposed to pornography and that many of them wanted legislation to make it illegal. Their general opinion was that it degraded women and gave men the idea that women were nothing but sex objects, to be used and abused in whatever way men wanted.

This is an ongoing sociosexual question I never intended this book to answer. But if we're going to discuss how to satisfy the secret sexual urges that practically all men feel, we have to ask ourselves whether you're right to satisfy them, or whether you will be prostituting yourself for love and affection and security, which you should expect from your man for nothing.

I have one unshakable rule about sex: both partners must enjoy everything they do together—*everything,* whether it's intercourse or mutual masturbation or dressing up in leather or whatever.

The rule of mutual enjoyment ensures the preservation of mutual respect and mutual dignity.

Sometimes—in the case of sadomasochistic sex, for example—the definition of "enjoyment" is definitely strained. Helen, twenty-four, told me, "My boyfriend liked to clip chrome clothespins on the lips of my vagina, with strings attached to the ends, so that when he tied the strings tight around my bottom, my vagina was pulled wide open. He used to push two or three lighted cigarettes up my anus, filter-first, of course, and I had to masturbate myself to an orgasm before he would take them out."

Sounds terrible, yes? Sounds extreme? But in this particular case, Helen confessed that she was just as excited by this pretense of degradation and humiliation as her boyfriend was—so long as she could always be sure that it *was* a pretense and so long as she remained 100 percent confident that her boyfriend would never actually hurt her. "He loved me. If he hadn't have loved me, I wouldn't have bothered. In any case, it was always a fantasy. You know, closing your eyes and masturbating, and having to keep your legs wide apart because those cigarettes were hot. But all the time knowing you could take them out yourself if you wanted to . . .

and that you didn't even have to have them in there in the first place.

"Let me tell you something: my boyfriend never punched me and he never slapped me—not once. He wasn't violent. He just enjoyed playing erotic games. There's nothing degrading about a man pegging your vagina wide open, so long as he loves you and you want him to do it. Sometimes I used to do the same kind of thing to him. I used to push a flashlight up his ass and switch it on. It was wild, I'll admit, but we were playing, that's all, we were discovering each other.

"I have plenty of friends who have really serious adult relationships—straight, honorable sex, plenty of dignity—but behind closed doors their husbands beat the shit out of them. Sometimes their husbands don't beat the shit out of them, but degrade them in other ways, like insulting their intelligence at dinner parties, or treating them like they're totally ugly and totally dumb, even when they're gorgeous and bright.

"You can keep relationships like that. To me, they're sadism, really. But in any case, you can never generalize. I'm living with a man who has a thing for kinky playacting, and if it turns him on, then I like it, too."

Most men have far less extravagant sexual urges than Helen's boyfriend. As we have seen from earlier chapters, oral sex comes first on the list of unfulfilled desires, followed by anal sex (not necessarily full anal intercourse), erotic clothing of one kind or another, and wet sex, of which more later.

Most men most of the time would be completely fulfilled by lovemaking that wasn't more outrageous, but simply more frequent. And occasionally spiced up with naughty panties, a sexy magazine or two (which you had bought), and a weekend together in a strange hotel, pretending to be honeymooners all over again.

You should already be an equal partner in your sex relationship. In fact, after reading this book, I expect you to be the more powerful partner. You can use your man's secret sexual desires to your own advantage, provided you aren't prudish, provided you're brave enough, and provided you accept that all men, no matter what they tell you, have the most erotic of fantasies.

Pornography is often blamed for men's sexual violence toward women. Men are quickly stimulated by pornography, and by pornographic fantasies, but my decade of experience in the erotic-magazine business taught me that sex movies and sex magazines are nothing more than a trade that makes a profit out of bringing men's frustrated fantasies to life. Looking at pornography will not turn an ordinary, decent man into a sex monster, any more than not looking at pornography will rehabilitate a man who is already brutish in his attitudes toward women.

A well-balanced man who has a close and satisfying sex relationship with the woman in his life will rarely feel any urge to look at pornography, except as an erotic titillation he and his partner can share together. If you do discover that your husband or lover is interested in pornography, you ought to take a close look at what kind of material he likes. It could give you important clues to what he thinks is missing in your own sex life.

It may not be obvious at first what turns him on. He may simply like to look at pictures of girls with no clothes on. In that case, you should try not to react in a negative way, and you certainly shouldn't feel jealous. He is reacting to visual sexual stimulation in the way that almost every man in the world reacts to visual sexual stimulation; he is not looking in real life for a girl who looks like any of the girls in the photographs.

As one therapist remarked, "Pornography is no more immoral than fashion magazines or car magazines or any publication that deliberately sets out to give its readers a vicarious thrill. The thrill is pleasurable, but ultimately empty."

The emptiness of pornography is demonstrated by the fact that men who enjoy it continually have to buy more to renew the thrill that it gives them, whereas you can go on thrilling him for years.

I am the first to defend women against sexual abuse or sexual degradation of any kind, no matter how subtle it may be. But in sexual relationships where both partners have respect for each other's feelings and sensitivities, where there is true friendship and true love, I am the first to believe that a woman should try to understand and accommodate her partner's frustrated sexual urges. Just as he should try to understand and accommodate hers, although that is another story, for another book.

We have to face the reality of human relationships; and the reality is that most marriages and long-term relationships break up for sexual reasons, and that one of the most common of these reasons is that the male partner feels unable to satisfy some of his most deeply suppressed desires.

I am also the first to believe that if women were to understand that their partners are almost certain to have at least one strong frustrated sexual desire—whether they will admit to it or not—and if they were to try to discover what it is, and to include it in their sex lives, then countless relationships would be happier, calmer, more fulfilled. There would also be fewer outbursts of pent-up sexual violence.

The same applies to men. Far too many husbands and so-called lovers leave their sex partners frustrated and angry and unfulfilled, without even realizing it.

This is Tina, a twenty-six-year-old dental nurse from Charleston, South Carolina: "I found out in a very roundabout way that Cy was turned on by black frilly underwear. He was looking through a copy of *Vogue* while he was waiting for me at the hairdresser, and there was a picture in it of girls wearing black stockings and garters and he asked me what I thought about that—you know, like he really thought it was sexy.

"I didn't think anything about it at all, not for months. There was no reason why I should have done, really. That wasn't the kind of underwear that I used to wear, not in a million years. Calvin Klein briefs were more my style. But then a girl at the clinic showed me a catalog of sexy underwear that she had borrowed from a friend, and asked me if I wanted to order any. I laughed my head off and said that I could never wear anything like that. I wasn't a stripper. But she said that her boyfriend absolutely went crazy for it.

"Well, I said, 'Don't you think it's kind of sleazy?' But she said, 'It turns him on, and we have a good time, that's all. There's nothing sleazy about that.'

"After she went home, I sneaked into her desk and looked through the catalog more slowly. I was amazed by some of the underwear. You know, G-strings and crotchless panties and peephole bras and even pantyhose with no crotch in them. And a whole lot of baby-doll nightdresses and garter belts.

"I thought of that time at the hairdresser and that picture in *Vogue*, and then I suddenly thought of all the times that Cy had said to me, your underwear reminds me of men's locker rooms. And I thought to myself, Maybe I'll try it. Because, you know, there was something about it that appealed to me, too, in a whorish kind of a way. I think every woman is a whore at heart, a little bit anyway; it's part of being a woman. I wrote down the address and sent away for a black G-string and a black garter belt, black stockings, and a black satin nightdress that left my breasts completely bare.

"I made sure I stuck around for the mailman every morning, just to make sure that Cy didn't get to my underwear first. The package took about three weeks to arrive, and by the time it did, I wasn't even sure that sexy underwear was a good idea anymore. But that evening, before Cy came home, I put on the G-string and the garter belt and the black stockings, under my skirt. I stood in front of the mirror with my skirt lifted up, and believe me, if I'd wanted to look whorish, I'd sure managed it.

"I was nervous, but I was excited as well. I kept walking up and down, and that G-string seemed to rub me right up between my legs, I didn't know whether it was sexy or irritating. I went and stood in front of the mirror again, and I pulled it up a little tighter. The next thing I knew I had slipped my hand underneath it and started masturbating. I hadn't masturbated for years, not since Cy and I had first started going out together, but that evening I was really carried away.

"I think it was something to do with the way that I was deliberately setting out to be sexual. I had dressed myself up with the specific intention of turning Cy on and having sex. I suddenly realized, too, that I was thinking about him in a way that I hadn't thought about him for a long, long time. I was thinking about him lustfully, I was thinking about him making love to me and about how excited he was going to be when he saw me dressed up like this.

"There was a little bit of fantasy in it, too, seeing myself in the mirror dressed up like a prostitute. I was kneeling down on the rug with my skirt twisted up around my waist, my G-string pulled to one side, and my fingers flying over my clitoris. When I climaxed, I cried out loud, and I hadn't done that for longer than I could remember."

What was Cy's reaction when he saw her dressed like that?

"He came into the living room, with his briefcase in his hand and his newspaper under his arm, and he couldn't understand what was happening at first, because I'd turned the lights down real low. I stood in the middle of the room. God, I was nervous! I was trembling, I was so nervous. He said, 'Hi, honey,' but all I said was 'Look,' and lifted up my skirt.

"He walked up to me and he was smiling from

ear to ear. He kissed me and he held me tight, and he said, 'You sexy thing, you!'

"He kissed me again and slipped his hand underneath my garters and then down inside the tops of my stockings.

"He said, 'You never dressed like this before.' And I said, 'Well, I felt like it. And I thought you might like it.'

"He said, 'Like it! You're sensational.' And that was the first time that he ever called me sensational, and I have to tell you that I liked the feeling of the man in my life calling me sensational.

"He slipped his hand up between my thighs. My pussy was all wet because I'd been masturbating, and I had pulled the G-string tight up between my pussy lips. He had to ease the G-string out with his finger and pull it to one side. Then he slid his finger up inside me and kept on kissing me. He called me a whole lot of lovely, dirty names.

"I could feel how hard he was, under his pants. I opened them up and took out his cock, and he felt enormous. I stroked him and rubbed him, and then he laid me down on the floor, right in the middle of the living room, in his business suit, and he lifted my legs right up in the air, and he fucked me so beautifully that I can remember it even now, I can still remember those actual feelings.

"I have quite a collection of sexy underwear now. Sometimes Cy buys me some, if he's feeling generous, or horny, or both. I have G-strings and quarter-cup bras and some really incredible playsuits. I don't wear them all the time. But if we're spending an evening at home watching television or listening to music, I usually dress up in something sexy for him. You see this playsuit? Nothing but a triangle of white lacy nylon with shoulder straps. It doesn't cover my breasts at all. I wore that all evening last week, even made dinner wearing it. Or this one . . . It covers up everything except my bottom.

"It's made us sexually more aware of each other. Cy certainly takes more trouble to make sure that he satisfies me. And it's brought fun back into our sex life. You know, like we're playing together again. I think a whole lot of couples should play more.

"I don't feel for one moment that it's degrading for a woman to wear erotic underwear. She's teasing and showing off her body, and if her husband likes her body as much as Cy likes mine, there's nothing degrading in it at all. And, besides, Cy says he wouldn't trade me for any other woman in the world, ever, and that's always good for a woman to hear."

The key to discovering your man's secret sexual desires is to try as many sexual variations as you can. Of course, that's easier said than done: many women are afraid of trying out some new sexual technique, because they're afraid that their partner may react with suspicion or even disgust. Men can be prudish, too! To have your partner rebuff you when you are trying to be sexually adventurous can be embarrassing, to say the least—even humiliating. But men feel just as cautious about putting their sexual desires into practice, and that is why so many secret sexual urges remain secret and why women who have the skill and the understanding to unlock them always succeed in pleasing their men.

Fortunately, there are subtle ways of discovering your man's private pleasures. I have yet to come across the man who does not relish the idea of his partner giving him oral sex—and as I have mentioned before, this is number one on the list of secret sexual desires. But some men may prefer your approach to oral sex to be indirect, and you yourself may wish to take your time when you try it, particularly if you are not very experienced in it.

You can first approach it by choosing a time when, for instance, he is lying in bed watching television or reading. Rest your head on his stomach and stroke his thighs and his stomach quite slowly and casually. Then, after a while, direct your attention to his testicles and his penis, manipulating them gently with your hands, until he becomes erect—if he isn't already.

This approach has several advantages. It is quiet and loving and gentle. It gives you the opportunity to study his erect penis closely, which surprisingly few women ever get—and when they do, surprisingly seldom). It gives him the opportunity to discontinue your caresses if he doesn't feel like them, although, as I have said, I have yet to come across the man who would. And it gives you the opportunity to discontinue your caresses if you change your mind.

In this position, you can kiss and lick his penis quickly and occasionally and casually at first. Then, if you wish, you can change your position and have intercourse with him, or you can continue to suck his penis for as long as you both enjoy it.

I have mentioned ejaculation before. Many women like to swallow their partner's semen when he ejaculates, and despite some old wives' tales that suggest that semen enlarges your breasts, it contains nothing but proteins and simple sugars and will have no effect on you whatsoever. If you don't like swallowing semen, there are plenty of alternatives, as we have seen. But it is most important that you do not react negatively to your partner's ejaculation. I have received a number of complaints from disconsolate husbands whose wives treated their sperm as if were "totally repulsive."

One husband wrote, "She gives me head and brings me off, and lets me shoot my cum all over her face. But immediately she makes a fuss of wiping it all with Kleenex and then going to the bathroom and washing her face and brushing her teeth and gargling with mouthwash. I'm beginning to feel like I'm some kind of patient, rather than a lover, and that my wife thinks, Oh, I have to do this, to be a good wife, but that doesn't mean I have to like it, or even that I have to pretend to like it. It has almost put me off oral sex totally. Why couldn't she just for once lie there afterward with the cum on her face and let me kiss her and share the experience?"

If you believe that your man may be aroused and fulfilled by ejaculating over your body or your face, and you wish to do it, then you can always experiment by pretending the first time it happens that it happened by accident, then touching it in surprise with your fingers and expressing pleasure.

The second most prevalent sexual urge that men suppress is the urge to make love to their partners anally. This is a sexual technique that you should only encourage if you derive unqualified sexual pleasure from it yourself. To be penetrated anally by a fully erect male penis when you are not in the mood for it can be extremely painful and offputting and even injurious.

These days, there is one overriding rule that must govern all sexual relationships, and particularly relationships in which the partners enjoy anal sex. Unless you are absolutely 101 percent sure that your partner is not a carrier of the AIDS virus, and unless you are absolutely 101 percent sure that your partner is completely sexual faithful to you, then you must insist that he wears a condom.

If you like anal sex—and a small proportion of women find it highly erotic and stimulating, once in a while—you can practice for it by inserting vibrators or dildos into your anus, making sure that you use a generous quantity of lubricant like KY jelly. You can buy vibrators that are specially made for anal insertion, sometimes with latex sleeves with protrusions or bumps on them to heighten stimulation. Several vibrators are designed like a Y-shaped cactus, so that they can be inserted into vagina and anus simultaneously.

After you have grown accustomed to the insertion of the more slender vibrators, you will find that you are able to graduate to the thicker variety. Anna, a pretty twenty-seven-year-old schoolteacher from New York, wrote to admit that she regularly enjoyed stimulating herself anally with a huge ten-inch vibrator, and was this kinky?

Hardly—when you consider that the anus is richly endowed with nerve endings and that rhythmic tugging on the anus has the same stimulating effect on the clitoris as vaginal intercourse.

Encouraging your man to try anal stimulation isn't difficult. It can introduce unexpected new variety into your sex life. This is Leda, a thirty-one-year-old computer programmer from San Diego: "Our sex life was just dull. It was like we couldn't interest each other anymore. I noticed that every time we went out to a party or to any kind of social gathering, Brett would spend a whole lot of time talking and flirting with other women. I began to feel that I was losing him. The truth of it was, you know, sexually, we just weren't getting it on. There was no spark there anymore.

"Then I was talking to a girlfriend of mine and she said she was dating a new man and what a total wow he was. She said they'd spent a fantastic night together. She said the only drag was, it was her period. I said, 'Didn't he mind?' But she said, 'Of course not, there are other ways of doing it,' and she patted herself on the fanny and said, 'That's why I can't sit down without saying ouch.'

"I was so dumb it took me five minutes to realize that she meant making love up the ass. I asked her about it again during our lunch break and did it really hurt and stuff like that. I guess I was shocked, but I was fascinated, too. She said that men really dug it. I said that Brett didn't dig it, he'd never even tried it. She said, 'You waggle your fanny at him, you'll see.'

"She said all I had to do was slip his cock out of me when we were making love the normal way, and press the head of his cock up against my bottom. If he didn't get the message and tried to put it back in my vagina again, I should go on slipping him out and pressing him up against my bottom until he realized what I wanted.

"She said that I should push myself downward, onto his cock, but the trick was to push with my bottom muscles at the same time, like I was trying to force something out of it rather than take it in. That way your bottom opens wider and you can get his whole cock up inside you without it hurting.

"I tried it about two nights later. We'd been out to a pretty slow party and decided to come home early. We went to bed and watched some television; then Brett turned me over and pushed his cock into me. He never believed in what-d'you-call-it, foreplay; with him it was straight in, and that was it. But this time I reached around behind him and took him out and held his cock up against my bottom, the way my friend had told me.

"He didn't know what was happening at first, but then I turned around and kissed him and said, 'Come on, fuck me.' So he tried to push it in.

"It wasn't easy at first. My first automatic reaction was to tighten my muscles instead of loosening them. But then he pushed again, and I pushed back, and the head of his cock pushed its way inside. It felt absolutely and totally enormous, as if it had grown ten times. Then he pushed again, and he was halfway in. One more time, and he was buried in my bottom right up to his balls. I could reach between my legs and feel him there.

"He made love to me real slow. When you make love like that, you can't slip in and out the way you do when you make love the usual way. Like it's too tight. But that slowed him down, and he liked it so much he wasn't in a rush anymore. He just churned that enormous cock of his around and around inside me, and it felt like the whole of my insides were being stirred.

"I felt more in control, too. I'd actually taken charge of our lovemaking, for a change. We were doing what I wanted to do, at the speed I wanted to do it. I took hold of his hand and cupped it around my breasts and showed him how I liked my nipples to be tugged. I really like them tugged, you know, stretched right out. And then I guided his hand down between my legs and showed him how to stroke me.

"He was totally awkward at first, but then he began to give me those gentle butterfly flicks, and that was wonderful.

"I was so turned on I was practically screaming. I wished I'd taken a mirror to bed, so that I could throw off the comforter and open up my legs and watch what was going on. I wanted to see it as well as feel it. I wanted to see my ass stretched open and I wanted to see his balls right up against my bottom. I wanted to see what I was doing to him, and what he was doing to me.

"For the very first time ever, I felt him come. I felt it like liquid spurting inside me. Then, I came too, and I came so violently that I hit my forehead against the side of the bed and practically knocked myself out. But it was incredible. Really incredible. We've done it a whole lot of times since, but that first time was truly special, believe me."

I have had many queries about the hygiene aspects of anal sex, especially from women who are hesitant to try it in case it's "dirty." They can be reassured that there is usually no fecal matter in the rectum, which is as far as the finger or the penis penetrates. On the other hand, however, the bowel is a virulent breeding-ground for bacteria, and common-sense precautions are essential. In particular, you should *never* allow your lover to return his penis or his finger to your vagina after anal sex without thorough washing first. And it cannot be repeated often enough: *never* risk anal sex with anyone, even your own husband, unless you have cast-iron proof that he is not HIV-positive.

Intelligently and sensitively performed, however, anal sex can introduce an entire new dimension to your sex life. As thirty-one-year-old Joy wrote to me, "It's doubled my pleasure, doubled my fun! I feel as if I have two vaginas now, and we never have to stop our very active lovelife for that 'time of the month.' "

In the erotic classic *The Story of O*, the girl O is required to wear "inserted in her anus and held in place by three little chains attached to a leather belt encircling her haunches, held, that is to say, in such a manner that the play of her internal muscles was unable to dislodge it, an ebonite rod fashioned in the shape of an uprisen male sex." The effect of wearing this, and increasingly larger and thicker rods as the days wore on, was to make sure that she was "doubly open."

Linda Lovelace claimed in her *Deep Throat* days that her anal apitude became so good that she was able to take two men up her anus simultaneously.

Even if you find full anal penetration too uncomfortable for you, you can still open yourself up to your lover's fingers, especially during intercourse, when his pleasure can be heightened by massaging his own penis through the thin wall of skin that separates vagina and rectum.

After oral sex, anal sex, and the wearing of erotic underwear, masturbation comes high on the list of men's hidden sexual urges. We have already discussed masturbation and masturbatory techniques in some detail, but it is worth remembering that one touch of your hand on your lover's penis is worth a million repetitions of the words "I love you."

Another often-suppressed urge is the desire to hear you talk dirty while you're making love. For many men, this is an extraordinarily powerful turn-on—and for many women, too. This is Janine, a twenty-three-year-old divorcée from Houston, Texas, who recently set up home with Larry, the prosperous proprietor of an auto mart, forty-two years old. Larry was married with three children when he met Janine at a sales convention, and their first night together was supposed to be a "one-night stand."

"But Larry went wild for the way I made love to

him. I love making love, there's no point in doing it if you don't love it, and I think you should show your man that you love it, too. You should throw yourself into it. When you're naked in bed together, that's no time to be shy and embarrassed. That's a special time, when there's nobody else around, and two people can share all the sexy thoughts that have been going around in their minds, and do all the things together that two people can possibly do together.

"I can never believe that some women just lie there and let their men do it to them and then turn over and go to sleep. I'm not sex-crazy or anything like that. You can ask my first husband whether I was a nymphomaniac or not, and he'll tell you no, I just liked ordinary regular loving like any other wife. But when I'm doing it, at least I do with enthusiasm. If you don't like the guy's hairy ass or you don't like his dick, then why go to bed with him?

"I always tell a man what I'm feeling, too, and what I want. I never talk dirty outside the bedroom, I don't even say darn. But when I've got my fist around Larry's great big stiff dick, I say things like, 'Look at this giant dick, I want it up my cunt so bad, I want you to fuck me so hard that I cry,' and all kinds of stuff like that. And I flatter him, and I tell him he's the greatest dirtiest filthiest fucker that ever fucked, you know the kind of thing, and it drives him wild. And I love to hear myself saying the words, because when you're having sex with the man you love they're dirty but they're not dirty, if you can understand what I'm saying.

"And Larry said his wife never spoke to him that way, not ever."

Eunice, twenty-five, from Butte, Montana, was more lyrical with her pillow talk, and she also used it to give the man in her life a running commentary on her body and how she felt when he touched it.

"I love to lie on the bed with my eyes closed while Jack touches me gently all over with his fingertips. It's so sensual, you have no conception. He runs his hands through my hair and gives me that tingly feeling in my scalp, and I tell him what that feels like. Then he touches my breasts and my nipples, and I say something like 'That's like soft electricity, it makes my breasts tingle, it makes my nipples feel as if they're longing to be touched some more.' He runs his hands all over me and makes me shiver. Then he opens up my vagina, and I let him touch and explore as much as he likes, saying things like 'Those are my lips; when you rub them like that between your finger and your thumb, that makes them feel thicker and fuller—and that's my clitoris, don't touch it like that, it makes me shudder. But you can slip your finger in there anytime.'

"Sometimes he pushes one of my long pearl necklaces inside my vagina, and gently draws it out again, pearl by pearl. Other times he uses his tongue, or other things, I have to lie with my eyes tight shut and guess what they are. It's something we do on a long weekend afternoon; it's a quiet kind of a turn-on, most of the time, but it brings us very close."

Eunice's game satisfied another secret sexual urge: the urge that many men feel to look at their partners closely, to be aroused with their eyes. Yet very few women feel comfortable when they are being examined so intently. It makes them feel vulnerable, and very much like a sex object. But they should at least try to understand that men adore looking at their women undressed, it's an integral part of the way in which men are aroused by women, and there is nothing clinical or detached or unloving in a man simply wanting to study and touch his partner's genitalia.

The strength of the male urge to do this is proved beyond doubt by the enormous multimillion-dollar industry in striptease, sexy videos, and explicit magazines. A woman in a photograph can be carefully studied without feeling suddenly embarrassed and closing her legs or protesting that she is not an anatomical diagram, but a real person.

A woman who understands her partner's erotic curiosity, however, and who can find a way to satisfy it, is a woman who is getting close to the very core of male sexual response, and a woman whom any man would find very hard to leave.

Jacqueline, a tall twenty-four-year-old sales assistant in a perfumery store in Philadelphia, with a remarkable figure, said she had learned early in her life that men like to look.

"It's their nature, isn't it? If I bend over a counter in a low-cut blouse, I'll catch the male customers trying to see my breasts. They all do it, whether they're old or young, whether they're respectable and old or cool and young. And that's why I like to play little games with my boyfriends, 'accidentally' leaving the bathroom door open so that they can see me in the mirror, or watch me in the tub through the crack in the door. Or else I'll clean the apartment in nothing but a T-shirt and bend over to pick things up from the floor so that they get a quick flash. Other times I'll come out of the shower to answer a phone call, and sit in the hallway drying myself while I'm talking on the phone, and I'll know darn well that they can see me from the landing. They always pretend that they haven't been looking. As soon as you try to catch their eye, the turn their heads away. They don't understand how natural it is. If I pulled up my skirt right now and pulled down my panties, I defy any man not to look."

Many women have already understood the very different nature of male sexuality and have used it in their sex lives to their own advantage.

You can say that men are sexually visual, that they respond very quickly if they see anything erotic.

You can also say that they are surprisingly cautious in many ways about initiating sexual acts, for fear of being rejected or of making fools of themselves, and they need their woman's reassurance and positive help much more often than they will ever admit. Thousands of marriage breakups are already waiting to happen all over the country: spring-loaded by pent-up sexual frustrations that a man has been too timid to express or a wife has been too complacent to understand. The longer an urge remains unfulfilled the more likely it is to become obsessive, and the more likely it is to lead to browbeating and even violence.

You can say that men have an urge to perform sexual acts that appear to assert their physical dominance over women. I know that many feminists will argue that oral sex, anal sex, voyeurism, masturbation, and various other erotic variations are characteristic of the male desire to degrade and dehumanize women. But, in general, this is simply not the case. An act of physical dominance, if it is caring and restrained and if the intention is to arouse rather than to inflict hurt or humiliation, can also be an act of great gentleness and love. We have seen that those women who make up their minds to enjoy their partner's sexual desires—or at the very least to give them a reasonable try—are frequently rewarded for their consideration several hundred times over.

5

How to Make His Erotic Fantasies Come True

Erotic fantasies come in all shapes and sizes. It is currently fashionable for women to claim that they do not have erotic fantasies. According to recent opinion polls in large-circulation women's magazines, anything between 75 percent and 86 percent of the nation's women have no erotic fantasies of any kind.

On closer investigation, none of these opinion polls has asked their interviewees to explain what they think an erotic fantasy is. An erotic fantasy does not have to be a Technicolor full-length feature crowded with a complete cast of naked men, all imagined in pin-sharp detail, complete with sound track. An erotic fantasy can be nothing more than a blurry sensation, a sexual stirring at a particular idea, or sound, or touch, or situation.

An erotic fantasy can be as subtle as the idea of wearing silk against bare skin ... of lying in the grass in the open air while your lover makes love to you ... of being watched from the anonymous window of an adjacent apartment house while you stand naked at your window ... of being kissed ... of driving through the rain in a black Mercedes with a brutally handsome man who will do anything for you, provided you do anything for him.

There is no doubt, however, that men do have more vivid and more narrative erotic fantasies. But like dreams that repeat themselves, these fantasies are often surprisingly unchanging, year after year.

Many men have a "trigger" fantasy that incorporates their strongest sexual urges, and when they are aroused, their minds will turn to this fantasy, seeking the stimuli that they know will increase their mental and physical excitement.

As I discussed in my book *How to Drive Your Woman Wild in Bed*, it is perfectly possible for a man to think himself into erection, excitement, and eventual climax, without any physical stimulus on his penis whatsoever. I'm not saying it's easy. It requires intense concentration and considerable practice, but it can be done.

Most men, with very much less concentration and with no practice at all, can think of something sexual that will at least give them an erection.

The point is that if you can discover the "trigger" fantasy that stimulates your man, you can have tremendous control over his sexual arousal. You can enhance his physical excitement by joining in his fantasy, embellishing it, becoming part of it. What you can do, in fact, is to make yourself indistinguishable from his most powerful sexual thoughts.

This is not at all as big-brotherish—or should I say big-sisterish—as it sounds. Your control can only ever be stimulating and benign. You can give him enormously heightened sexual pleasure, and at the same time you will reap the benefits of his appreciation and his excitement.

"My wife doesn't understand me," is the oldest cliché in the book of broken marriages. But it still has a sour note of truth. Because so many women don't understand so many men, particularly when it comes to their sexual desires, and so many men can't find it in themselves to articulate what it is that they want.

There are many ways of discovering what special fantasies fire up your man's erotic imagination. But you must remember before you start to explore his innermost sexual imaginings that these are fantasies; they do not necessarily bear any relation to any-

thing that he would really like to do, in real life—
and they may be of shocking sexual intensity.

If you genuinely wish to find out what your man's
fantasies are, in order to improve your sex life, you
will have to make up your mind in advance that
you are going to accept them without question when
you discover what they are—no matter how bizarre
or extreme they turn out to be. If you're the squea-
mish kind, you'd be better off leaving well enough
alone.

If your man has erotic fantasies about making
love to underage girls, that doesn't mean that he's a
latent pederast. If he has erotic fantasies about
being whipped, that doesn't mean that he's a masochist. If he daydreams about dressing up in wom-
en's clothing, that doesn't make him a transvestite.

These are fantasies, that's all. Not hopes, not
expectations, not even wishes, but provocative sexual situations that the mind conjures up in order to
heighten sexual excitement.

After they have climaxed, many men look back
on what they were thinking immediately prior to
ejaculation, and they feel ashamed of themselves,
although their thoughts were quite normal, and they
have no need to be.

You have no need to worry, either, that your
man's erotic fantasies in any way reflect his true
personality.

This is Olive, thirty-two, from Cleveland, Ohio.
Olive was recently married to Charles, a thirty-
four-year-old insurance executive who left his wife
for her. "We were lying in bed one evening and we
were talking about Charles' first wife, and whether
he ought to go back to her. Charles said he didn't
want to go back, but he felt guilty about deserting
her; she hadn't done anything actually wrong. She'd
always been the loyal and faithful wife, good cook,
good friend. She couldn't have children, but that
hadn't put him off. They'd already decided to adopt
one day.

"The only trouble was, one night, after he'd had

a few drinks, he'd confessed his biggest sexual fantasy to her. He'd thought, you see, that it would turn her on, as much as it turned him on, but of course it didn't. She'd been utterly shocked.

"Their sex life had never been the same after that. She'd been cold and reserved and really made him feel like he was a pervert.

"I asked him what his fantasy was, but he refused to tell me at first. In the end, though, after a whole lot of cajoling, he came out with it. He'd always had a fantasy about dressing up in women's underwear. He wasn't gay, he wasn't a transvestite, he wasn't any of that, the idea of it just turned him on.

"Apparently he'd suggested to his wife that the next time they made love, he should try wearing a pair of her stockings and a garter belt. Well, as I say, she'd gone crazy. She hadn't tried to understand him at all. She hadn't been able to see that it was just a turn-on for him, that's all, a let's-pretend."

But how had Olive felt about it? Had she been at all shocked?

"No, I wasn't shocked. I don't really think that I was even surprised. Charles had always been a very strong personality, but he's quiet, you know? And he's sensitive, too. I think he has a feminine element in him, like a lot of men do, although they won't admit it, not for a moment."

So what did she do?

"I did what instinctively I thought was the right thing to do. I got him to talk about his fantasy, tell me about it. I talked about some of my sexy ideas, too, just to make him understand that women have fantasies, too. I mean, one of my biggest fantasies is standing in a huge jostling crowd in the street to watch a parade go past, and some totally strange unknown man lifts up my skirt at the back and makes love to me. I never find out who it is. I look around and all the men in the crowd look the same, and none of them gives me so much as a smile.

"Charles told me that he had started having this

fantasy six or seven years ago, when he had seen a photograph in a magazine of a man wearing black stockings. It was something in *Esquire*, I think, about men as sex objects. Somehow it had stuck in his mind. When he was feeling horny, he thought about wearing stockings himself, and women's panties, too. He fantasized that he was hired to model women's underwear for one of those underwear parties they have in women's homes—you know, the ones like Tupperware parties.

"The climax to his fantasy was that the women all fondled him and masturbated him. I played up to his fantasy. I couldn't see any harm in it. Where was the harm? One Saturday afternoon when we were lying around the house after lunch, I said to him, 'You know that fantasy of yours, when you dress up in women's underwear?' And he said, 'Y-e-es,' kind of suspicious. I said, 'Why not do it? You can try on some of my underwear.'

"I think Charles was a little anxious at first. He thought he was going to make himself look ridiculous. But we went through to the bedroom, and I opened up my closet and took out a pair of stockings and a garter belt and several different pairs of panties. Then Charles undressed and I helped him to try them on.

"He stood in front of the mirror, wearing black stockings and a tiny little pair of black nylon panties. I stood behind him and reached inside his panties and took out his cock and slowly masturbated him. All the time I was saying things like, 'And here, ladies, is a provocative little pair of black briefs, trimmed with lace . . .' as if I was holding one of those parties he had always imagined.

"Then I got him to change into different panties . . . a pair of white French step-ins, and some bright scarlet briefs, and then one of my bikinis that I always wear under white slacks. His cock was so hard by then that he couldn't even get it into the panty. I kept on masturbating him in the mirror, but then he turned me around, so that I was bent forward over the bed, and he lifted up my dress and pulled my panties to one side, and without any kind of preliminaries he pushed his cock right up inside me.

"It was strange, feeling a man's legs in nylon stockings, right up behind me. But it was a turn-on, too, because we were doing something different and private and maybe you could call it forbidden, too, if you know what I'm trying to say. You don't always want your sex life to be pure and clean and proper. Sometimes you want to feel that you're doing something really dirty and wicked.

"I guess my fantasy—you know, my fantasy of having a strange man make love to me in a crowd was partly fulfilled, too, because Charles was very fierce, very strong, and he didn't feel like Charles at all. I was so turned on that I was beating my fists on the bedcover and shouting out loud. His cock was so rigid, I'd never felt it so rigid before. It seemed to go so far up inside me I thought it was going to come out of my mouth.

"We both climaxed together, which was something we hadn't done in a coon's age. It was just amazing. Talk about stars and fireworks. Amazing.

"Afterward, I think Charles felt embarrassed, lying on the bed in stockings and panties. He started to take them off, but I told him not to, I said to keep them on for a while. I think that was the right thing to do. It showed him that his fantasy didn't upset me after everything was all over. And so *he* didn't feel so bad about it, either."

What were Olive's conclusions about Charles' dressing-up games?

"He dresses up very rarely these days. But he knows that if he feels like it, we can do it, I won't be disgusted and I won't think that he's weird. I think it's incredible that so many couples live together and they can't discuss some of the most secret and important thoughts that go on inside of their heads, because it could ruin their marriage. Our sex life is very strong, our relationship is very strong. I think Charles knows that if he had a fantasy about anything, he could talk to me about it."

And her advice to wives?

"A fantasy is only a fantasy. You shouldn't be frightened of it. Finding out what your husband's fantasy is, and discussing it—well, that could be the one thing that makes your marriage better than ever, forever. Let me put it this way: it's better that your man plays out his fantasies with you than if he tries to play them out with somebody else."

A desire to wear women's underwear is not at all uncommon, even in men of complete sexual normality. It is quite distinct from the psychological need that some men have to dress up in skirts and wigs and cosmetics and behave as a woman might do.

The underwear fantasy is an attempt to feel the excitement of sex from the woman's point of view, to enjoy the pleasures of both sexual roles at once. Considering that one of the great delights of sexual intercourse is when a man and a woman feel that they have become one, this fantasy is quite comprehensible, and not at all strange.

However, it also has some connections with the sexual desire that many men feel from time to time that they would like their women to dominate them—sexually, at least. Even the most masculine of men has some submissive aspects in his sexual personality, and can be erotically excited by feeling helpless in the hands of an unforgiving woman.

I went to The Hague in Holland to talk with Monique von Cleef, the notorious Dutch dominatrix, whose "house of sexual correction" featured such sadomasochistic gadgets as spiked penis muzzles, racks, pillories, and a three-legged milking stool on which her clients would be forced to sit while she told them nursery stories. Protruding from the center of the milking stool's seat was a huge wooden phallus.

Miss von Cleef was quite clear why her business

was such a success. Many men in important jobs in industry or public service would feel the need sometimes to be responsible for nobody and nothing, almost to be treated like babies again. They would like to be whipped, tied up, given forced enemas. And they would visit her for their "punishment" because they were unable to explain their erotic fantasies to their wives.

"Their wives simply would not understand. They would be horrified. Yet, if they could take the trouble to understand, there would be no need for places like mine."

Jane, a twenty-eight-year-old community worker from San Francisco, discovered a huge portfolio of drawings by her forty-one-year-old husband Ted, all of them showing men being chained and gagged and flagellated by severe-looking women, many of whom resembled her.

Unable to keep her discovery to herself, she confronted him with them and asked him if that was what he secretly wanted her to do to him.

"He said no. He said he was perfectly happy, that drawing those erotic drawings was just like a hobby. It was something that happened inside his own head, that was all.

"But I couldn't get the images out of my mind. The same image, over and over, a man tied up, a woman whipping him or torturing him. It didn't seem like Ted at all. He was so easygoing, so straightforward. He smoked a pipe, for God's sake.

"But one night, when we were lying together in bed, I reached over and started to stroke his bare chest—then, out of curiosity, to see how much pain he really could stand, to tweak his nipples. Then I sat astride his stomach and bit his nipples so hard that I drew blood.

"He winced, but he didn't cry out. So I said, 'You're helpless now, you're my prisoner and I'm going to punish you.'

"I did to him whatever I felt like. I have to tell

you, it gave *me* quite a kick, too. I kissed him and bit his lips and his tongue. I bit his neck and covered it with hickies. I scratched his chest and his stomach with my fingernails. And all the time I kept on saying, 'You're helpless, do you understand? You've been bad, and now you're going to be punished.'

"I took hold of his cock and squeezed it hard. I'd never dared to do that before. I'd hardly even dared to touch it. But now I realized that he liked me taking charge, he *liked* me hurting him. I dug my nails right into the shaft of his cock and then I bent down and nipped the skin all the way down the side of it with my teeth until he cried out.

"In the end, I was just as excited as he was. But I didn't let him take control. When he tried to turn me over onto my back, I shouted at him, 'You're my prisoner, you stay right where you are, you're chained up.' And he did, without a murmur. He was usually so assertive in bed, I couldn't even believe I was making love to the same man.

"I straddled him and held his cock tight in my hand and made him beg for me to put it inside me. I sat right up and positioned the head of his cock so that it nestled right between the lips of my pussy, and I said, 'Beg me to sit down.' And only when he'd begged me and begged me, and promised me all kinds of things like he'd clean the house for me Saturday and make love to me twice a day every single day for the next three months—only then did I slowly sit down. And sitting down on that long hard cock was such a pleasure, I can't describe it. I rode slowly up and down on it, as slowly as I wanted, and when I felt he was close to coming, I stopped riding up and down and teased him.

"He had a tremendous climax almost immediately afterward. I'd never heard him shout out like that before. But I hadn't reached an orgasm, not nearly, so I shifted myself up the bed and knelt over his face, and said, 'That's it, prisoner, you have to make sure that you satisfy me, too.'

"He kissed and licked my pussy until I could hardly bear it. His tongue was right up inside me, his own sperm was trickling down the sides of his mouth. But right then, he was my slave, he was my prisoner, and whatever I wanted him to do, that's what he had to do.

"We didn't talk about it afterward; we don't talk about it very much now; we don't have to; but we both feel a new closeness. How can I describe it? We both feel that our marriage has become more bonded. The big step for me was accepting that Ted's fantasies about whipping and being chained up were only fantasies, that's all. We don't use real chains, we don't use real whips. Ted does like to make believe that he's a prisoner, and he does enjoy the pain of being bitten and scratched, it really arouses him, but he doesn't enjoy it all the time, he wouldn't like that routine every single night of our married lives, no way. It's a part of his personality that has to let itself out, now and again, usually when he's stressed at work or if he feels that he's been underachieving.

"There's no harm in occasionally playing make-believe sex games. It's better than finding out that your husband is going to prostitutes to get his kicks, or to other women. I feel a new freedom, too, because if there's something I want Ted to do for me, whether it's sexual or not, I feel I have all the right in the world to ask him, and I think he feels that, too.

"Being totally truthful with each other has brought us new responsibilities, I think. But it's brought us much more security, much more certainty. I know who Ted is. He knows who I am. There's nothing hidden."

Sometimes, of course, a man may have fantasies of tying up and "raping" the woman in his life. Keeley, a thirty-one-year-old supermarket supervisor from Indianapolis, Indiana, sensed a taste for "rough sex" when she first went to bed with Gordon, a thirty-year-old computer salesman.

"He was very gentle most of the time, gentle and courteous and slow, but when he came close to his climax, he turned me over so that he was making love to me from behind. He gripped one arm around my neck and the other arm tight around my waist, and he pushed himself into me harder and harder, really banging me. I could hardly breathe, and I tried to pull his arm away from around my neck, but I couldn't. He was too strong.

"I was glad when it was all over. I felt like he'd tried to rape me."

Eventually, Gordon admitted to Keeley that the idea of tying her up and making love to her forcibly was one that really excited him. He had tried to persuade his live-in girlfriend, Samantha, to do it, but in Gordon's own words, Samantha was "chicken."

Keeley cautiously agreed, but made the following stipulations: that Gordon would never try to choke her, the way that he had almost choked her the first time they had made love. Second, that if she asked to be untied, he would do so right away, without argument. And, third, that he never leave her alone while she was helpless.

Keeley's conditions were based on the common-sense rules of bondage that I have repeated again and again. A little mild bondage can be stimulating, but not if it ends in hostility or exposes either partner to unnecessary risk.

Keeley actually enjoyed her bondage sessions with Gordon. "I guess you could say that I have a little touch of the masochist in me somewhere."

The first time, he tied her wrists and ankles to the head and the foot of the bed, gagged her with a scarf, and kissed her naked body all over while she lay helpless to stop him. Then he had intercourse with her, twice in quick succession.

"It was something I'd never experienced before, actually being inside a man's sexual fantasy, acting it out. I felt weird but also very sexually excited." When she returned home that night, she thought about it over and over. "I think what excited me most of all was the sensation of being helpless, but at the same totally wanted. I thought, This man is tying me up only because he wants me so much that he's frightened of letting me go.

The next time, Gordon hog-tied Kelley naked in the kitchen and forcefully had sex with her on the tiled floor. "I was cold, I was uncomfortable, I was completely naked. He made love to me and then he knelt down beside me and pushed his penis into my mouth and ordered me to suck it clean for him. I'd never come across anything like this before. I didn't know whether to be excited or frightened. But he was so careful and so loving, and every time we made love he took me out to dinner afterward and bought me flowers, so that I felt like I was doing something special for him. I was making his dream come true.

"He said he had suggested bondage to his girlfriend just twice. The first time she had flatly said no, the second time she had threatened to leave him.

"One time he took me out into the yard at the back of his house and tied me up against one of the porch posts, naked, right out there in the open air. If anybody had come around to the back of the house, they would have seen me easy. He made love to me standing up. When he was finished, I said he was going to have to let me go, I needed the bathroom. He said, 'Go ahead, this is where you're tied up, this is where you're going to stay.' He stood there kissing me and fondling my breasts, and I told him, 'I have to go.' He said, 'You can do it right here.'

"In the end, I couldn't hold it any longer, so I did. Gordon stepped up close and kissed me, and at the same time held his hard cock in between my legs, right in the stream of fresh pee that was coming out of me, massaging his cock all the time, washing it in my pee. When I was finished, he kissed me, and kissed me again, and said that I was the most fantastic girl ever, he had never met any girl like me. I had made all of his wildest fantasies come true.

"Yes, I think that a lot of women feel threatened by male sexual fantasies, especially by something like bondage. None of my friends believes me when I say that I don't feel endangered by Gordon tying me up. He wouldn't hurt me for anything, he loves me. He left his girlfriend only three weeks after we met, and he'd been living with her for nearly six years. Bondage makes me feel totally dependent, totally helpless, that's all, totally at Gordon's mercy, and that's what makes it exciting. My heart beats faster, I wonder what he's going to do next, whether he's going to bring me candies or kiss me or make love to me. Once he tied me up in the bath and peed all over my stomach and between my legs. I don't have any say in what he does, I let him indulge whatever fantasy he wants to. But then it's my fantasy to be treated that way, so we're both satisfied. And if ever the time comes when I've had enough, or he does something to me that I don't like, then I can say, 'Untie me,' and that's the end of it, he always does."

Despite the pleasure Keeley derived from satisfying Gordon's fantasies of bondage, I cannot emphasize too strongly that you should never attempt bondage with a man you don't already know and implicitly trust, that both of you understand the ground rules of what he can and can't do to you, and that you strictly adhere to the common-sense safety rules at all times.

It was interesting that Keeley mentioned two acts of what is popularly called "wet sex," or the inclusion of urination in lovemaking. Since I mentioned wet sex in *More Ways to Drive Your Man Wild in Bed*, I have received more queries and correspondence about this topic than almost any other, with the exception of temporary impotence and difficulties in achieving orgasm.

A great many men harbor fantasies about watching their wives or girlfriends urinate, or actually having them urinate over their genitalia or even their faces; or doing the same to their wives or girlfriends in return. The fantasy is obviously much more common than the fact, but Ellie, a twenty-six-year-old teacher from Sacramento, California, told me that she had discovered her husband, William's, secret desire for wet sex purely by accident.

"One night, when we were making love, I was sitting on top of William, he went really deep inside me, and I had truly extraordinary feelings. When I reached orgasm, though, I suddenly squirted out a little jet of pee. I was desperately embarrassed, but almost immediately William reached his orgasm, too. I apologized for what had happened, but William said that the sudden sensation of wetness on his testicles had been incredibly arousing. He said he would love me to do it again.

"For a long time, I didn't. Well, I wouldn't, I didn't want to. But one day we went camping together so that we could try out William's new boat. That night was wonderfully warm, and we lay on a blanket outside, looking up at the stars and drinking wine. Then we started to make love. It was romantic and relaxing and wonderful, but I guess I'd been drinking too much wine, because the same thing happened. This time, though, while he was still right up inside me, William said, 'Let it go, let it all go,' and so I just let it all gush out.

"After that, I knew how much he liked it, and so we started to do it more often. Sometimes I crouch over him and hold myself open with one hand and rub his penis with the other hand while I pee all over his testicles. Sometimes I lie back and hold myself wide apart while he pees right into my vagina. Or my favorite feeling is to hold his cock right up close to my nipples while he pees like a hot geyser all over them.

"As a teacher, I thought at first that to be excited

by wet sex had to be immature or unbalanced, or a sign of some sexual aberration. But when I discussed it with my best and closest friend, she said that she envied me. Her husband is something of a stuffed shirt when it comes to sex, and she wouldn't have dared suggest it to him, even though she found the idea of it arousing. She said that when her husband is away on extended business trips and she masturbates in the shower, she frequently pees over herself as part of her masturbation. Surely we can't all be aberrant!"

I have received dozens more questions and inquiries and intimate personal experiences, but perhaps it is enough to say that wet sex and curiosity about wet sex is very widespread—widespread enough to be the main theme for several regularly published American and European magazines and numerous erotic videos. Although some sexual pundits regard wet sex as immature—the thrill of doing something "dirty"—more modern research connects it with the way in which all animals attract their mates.

Each man has widely different sexual fantasies and different combinations of sexual desires. Discovering exactly what fantasies appeal to your man the most will be a matter of careful questioning, cajoling, teasing, tempting, trial and error, but if you can come up with a profile of what stimulates him the most, then you will be more than halfway toward being the kind of woman he won't be able to bear to be without.

I undertook a survey of all the men who have written to me over the past fifteen years, and the male partners of all those women who have written to me over the past fifteen years. The results cannot be judged as a scientific analysis of the nation as a whole, since people who write about their sexual interests are not typical of the population at large. But it did give me a fascinating profile of the principal topics of interest among those men who have a strong and specific interest in sex.

I asked them to describe the main erotic theme behind their most stimulating sexual fantasy. Arranged as a Top Ten of male sexual interests, the results came out as follows:

1) Nudity   The theme of female nudity in unusual surroundings was by far the most common theme running through male sexual fantasies. For instance, "flying on a 747 and peeping through the galley curtain and seeing a stewardess naked except for her high-heeled shoes and her airline cap," or "attending a formal dinner where the women are all beautifully dressed and coiffed, but their gowns are somehow pinned open at the front to expose them," or "imagining my wife walking around the house all day naked," or "watching young big-breasted girls playing volleyball, completely nude except for white sox and sneakers and peaked sun-visors."

2) Breasts   Almost 63 percent of men regularly had fantasies that revolved around seeing or touching or caressing a woman's breasts. In almost all of the fantasies, the breasts that were fantasized about were in the 40DD league. Such as "I imagine this very pretty young brunette, in shorts and a striped tank top, waiting for a train at my local station. She's very petite, but she has absolutely huge breasts—so much so that I can feel myself getting real excited. The train arrives and I'm just about to step up after her when the train conductor closes the door in my face, and says, 'Too young for what you've got in mind, mister. She's only twelve.' That makes my erection even harder. Imagine being only twelve and having enormous breasts like that!" Or "I'm watching this Mexican girl at a market stall, serving out fruit, and she's wearing one of those off-the-shoulder blouses, so that every time she bends forward to pick up fruit, I can see her bare breasts." Or "I'm fighting in the jungle someplace, it's incredibly hot. My companion is a blond Amazon-type woman about thirty. She's very fit,

very strong. She cuts her way through the jungle wearing nothing but these tight camouflage shorts. She has fantastic breasts, big and firm and smeared in sweat and gun grease. Her nipples are small and pink and stick up like .38-caliber bullets."

3) Genitalia   A high proportion of men (58 percent) reported having fantasies about women exposing their genitalia. "I'm standing on the roof of this building, and I happen to look down, through this window, and I can see this girl lying back on a couch. I can't see her face, but she lifts up this short floppy gray skirt, and underneath it she's naked, her pussy completely hairless. She starts to play with herself, stretching her lips, massaging her clitoris, pushing her fingers in and out. I'm watching all this, with my eyes wide, right, when she suddenly lifts up her head so that I can see her. She's incredibly pretty, blond hair, blue eyes. She smiles at me and blows me a kiss, and I take that for an invitation." Or "I'm attending some kind of class—math or physics, I think—and we're being taught by a very tall broad-shouldered woman—kind of Latin, I think. I like my women dark, with lots of black curly hair. Anyway she bends over in the aisle between the desks, and just for one split second I glimpse her cunt, crimson and shiny, with thick black hair, and then I have to spend the rest of the class pretending that I haven't, and that my cock isn't trying to burst its way out of my jeans."

To digress for a moment, it is interesting to note that the three most popular fantasies were mainly visual—fantasies about seeing women naked, fantasies about looking at a woman's bare breasts, and fantasies about catching glimpses of women's vulvas. My research into women's sexual psychology has shown that, unlike men, women fantasize almost exclusively about feelings and emotions and about acts, rather than seeing graphically sexual pictures in their mind's eye.

If you can bring yourself to understand that your man's most immediate sexual responses are primarily visual—if you can appreciate that the man in your life, if he really likes you, is sexually triggered by the way you look—then you will always have a secret weapon to keep your man interested in you.

Undress—or partially undress—at unexpected times of the day. When he's Black-and-Deckering in the workshop, bring him a cup of coffee topless, wearing nothing but shorts or jeans. When you're staying at home for the evening, watching television, borrow one of his shirts, but make sure you're naked underneath—and show him you're naked underneath. Sleep naked, do your household chores naked, not every day, but anytime you feel like it, and anytime you feel that your sex life might be flagging.

If he wants to touch you, let him. If he wants to make love to you, let him. It's a simple-enough formula for keeping your sex life alive, but out of all the complicated sexual fantasies that men have talked to me about, one overriding sexual interest stands out a mile beyond the rest.

Men like looking at naked women. It's no more mystifying than that. The most discerning of men will stare wide-eyed at a woman even if she works on the checkout at Lucky and thinks that everything printed in *The Star* is true. She doesn't even have to be particularly pretty. Provided, of course, she's naked.

You have a power over the man in your life, a power that will keep him faithful and satisfied and happy. That power is you, the woman he married, the woman he forgets to look at anymore. The answer is, Make him look. Make yourself the stuff of his fantasies. You don't have to perform like a hooker or a stripper, in the way that some "how-to" books recommend. You can keep up his interest and his excitement with occasional "accidental" glimpses, with spontaneous words of love and affection, and by never being too cautious to take the sexual initiative.

Let's go on and consider more popular male fantasies.

4) Exhibitionism   Or making love in front of other people. Very few men would really like to have intercourse with their wives while other people looked on, but the idea of it is a surprisingly strong erotic fantasy. "I picture that I'm sitting on a chair, in a roomful of people, and Jane is sitting naked on my lap, with her legs wide apart, and everybody can see my penis going in and out of her." Or "We're being photographed for a sexy magazine. Louise is sucking my cock, and the photographer comes right up close, focusing on her face just inches away." This fantasy can be partially realized by making love in front of a mirror, or by taking videos of your lovemaking and then watching them afterward.

5) Unusual locations   Having sex in the great outdoors, or in the sauna, or in your host's bathroom halfway through a dinner party. "Bill has always been turned on by the idea of making love in the back seat of the car. I don't know whether his first experience of sex was in a car, but he kept on suggesting it. In the end we did it, although the car was still in the garage at the time." Or "I often have fantasies about making love to a girl while she's standing up against a door or a wall, in the street. I just hitch up her skirt and pull her panties to one side and start fucking her."

6) Sadomasochistic sex   Even those men who wouldn't think of hurting their wives for one single moment, and who wouldn't actually enjoy being hurt themselves, can be turned on by the thought of sadomasochistic sex. "I used to have a recurring fantasy of having my cock strapped tight with leather thongs, and a huge dildo forced up my ass." Or "I imagine being tied up by seven or eight women, who force me to have sex with them again and again, and who go on rubbing and tugging at my cock long after I've lost the ability to get it up again."

7) Group sex   The idea of making love to more than one woman at a time, or of sharing a bed with other women and other men. "What really turns me on is this one particular fantasy of going to bed with twin girls—the thought of having intercourse with one of them while the other one kisses and strokes us and fondles us." Or "Having a sexy tussle on a waterbed with another couple, holding the other man's cock and guiding it into the other woman's pussy." Or "There's two of us, two guys, and just one woman, and I'm making love to the woman from the front while the other guy is pushing his cock up her ass, and our balls are banging against each other's, and then we both climax into her at one and the same time, and she's just screaming with delight."

8) Oral sex   Particularly for those men whose wives or girlfriends are reluctant to participate in oral sex, fantasies about having their penises kissed and sucked are of course very common and very stimulating. But although a desire to be fellated was the clear number one among men's secret sexual urges, I found that their fantasies about oral sex predominantly revolved around watching girls giving each other oral sex or about giving oral sex themselves to their wives or girlfriends or some fantasy woman. "I'm sitting in the college library. There's a very beautiful dark-haired girl sitting opposite me, she's wearing spectacles and a charcoal-gray suit. I slide beneath the table and put my head up inside her skirt. She's wearing stockings and the bare skin of her thighs clasps my cheeks. I open up her pussy with my fingers and start licking her. She's already slippery with juice." Or "Sometimes I have a fantasy about a tropical beach, and there are two girls on it, one black and one white, both amazing looking and both naked. While I'm watching them from the undergrowth, they sixty-nine each other. I can see their tongues slipping right inside their cunts." Naturally, if your husband or

lover has fantasies of this nature, they won't be difficult for you to fulfill.

9) Forcible sex   Some men have fantasies about violent or forcible sex that almost amounts to rape. Fantasies of this kind are comparatively common and do not necessarily mean that your lover would ever be inclined to rape anybody, you included. Much more often than not, they are simply an expression of aggressive male sexual urges. However, if the man in your life does show a strong interest in rape fantasies, be extremely careful about fulfilling them for him. Make sure that you known him well, that you trust him implicitly, and that an enactment of rough-and-tumble sex is with your consent and your enjoyment. "I'm always turned on by the thought of tearing open a girl's blouse and seeing her bare breasts burst out of it." Or "Just doing it, just getting down on the floor right then and there and doing it, no preliminaries, nothing, my cock sticking out of my pants and her legs up around my shoulders, still wearing her high-heeled shoes."

10) Masturbation   Fantasies of being intimately touched by women. Two of the most often-repeated male masturbation fantasies are (a) a fantasy of being masturbated while driving a car; and (b) a fantasy of being masturbated in the shower. I have no idea quite why these two scenarios should be so popular, but both of them should be comparatively simple for you to fulfill, although for safety's sake I must recommend that your vehicle should be stationary before you attempt to stimulate its driver. "I'm sitting in my car at a stoplight, right next to another car, and my girlfriend has my cock out, and she's jerking it like crazy. Suddenly there's sperm flying everywhere, and the people in the other car don't even know what's happened, or why I'm smiling." Or "We're showering together, and she starts pulling me off, real slow and easy, so slow and easy that I can hardly bear it. At last I shoot off, and it

spurts all over her stomach and runs down into her pubic hair. She smooths it around and around, all over her stomach, as if it's soap."

Now that you're aware of the ten most common male erotic fantasies, you can set about constructively discovering which of them triggers off the man in your life. It may be one particular fantasy, or a combination of fantasies, and it will almost certainly be colored by individual sexual nuances of his own.

How do you actually do it? Through a combination of discreet questioning and positive actions. For instance, you can discover how responsive he is to masturbation fantasies by actually masturbating him and at the same time describing an erotic situation to match your actions. Such as "Wouldn't it be fabulous if I could come around to your golf club one day and hide in the locker room, and while all your friends were showering, I could have a shower with you and massage your cock, and none of them would know."

Erotic fantasy is crucial to male sexual stimulation, and wives who are shocked by it or who would prefer not to think about it are ignoring their husbands' sexual needs at their own peril.

They are also depriving themselves of considerable stimulation and satisfaction, since a very high proportion of men fantasize about their existing partners, rather than other women or completely imaginary women. By taking the trouble to discover what turns their men on most, they will be able to participate actively in sexual scenarios that, up until now, were played out only in their partners' imagination.

Questionnaire—Discover Your Man's Secret Sexual Fantasies

Ask the man in your life to answer the following questions as truthfully as he can.

1) Whenever possible, I would like my wife/girlfriend to remain naked   YES/NO
2) I am highly sexually stimulated by the sight of my wife's/girlfriend's breasts   YES/NO
3) I wish my wife/girlfriend would expose herself sexually to me more often   YES/NO
4) I wish she would wear erotic clothing   YES/NO
5) I like the idea of going to bed with more than one woman   YES/NO
6) I like the idea of going to bed with one woman and another man   YES/NO
7) It would excite me to watch two women making love   YES/NO
8) I would like to tear off my wife's/girlfriend's clothes   YES/NO
9) I am excited by the idea of forcing a woman to have sex   YES/NO
10) I would like to make love in different places (such as outdoors, in the car, etc.)   YES/NO
11) I like the idea of my wife/girlfriend inflicting pain on me when we make love   YES/NO
12) I would like her to masturbate me more often   YES/NO
13) I like the idea of being helpless at the hands of several women   YES/NO
14) I would find it arousing to make love in front of an audience   YES/NO
15) I would be excited by somebody taking photographs of my lovemaking   YES/NO
16) I wish my wife/girlfriend were more responsive to oral sex   YES/NO
17) If she indicated that she enjoyed it, I would give her oral sex at any time of the day or night, and as often as she wanted it   YES/NO
18) I wish she would give me oral sex whenever I felt like it   YES/NO
19) I have a very strong recurrent sexual fantasy   YES/NO

20) I wish that I could tell my wife/girlfriend
    what my fantasy is   YES/NO

There are clearly no "right" or "wrong" answers to
this questionnaire, but by evaluating your man's
score of YESes and NOs and relating them to the
ten most popular male fantasies earlier in the chapter, you will find that you have the beginnings of a
clear profile of the kind of stimuli that appeal to
him the most.
    The rest is up to you!

6

Ask Not What You Can Do for Your Man ...

As we have seen, one of the most common complaints I receive from discontened husbands is that their wives never seem to take the sexual initiative. Because of this, they begin to think that perhaps their wives don't really care for sex all that much, and they try less and less often to initiate sex themselves.

The result, of course, is that the wife begins to believe that she is no longer as sexually attractive to him as she once was, and what you have is the thin end of a wedge that can lead to sexual disaffection, tensions, arguments, and even divorce. You would never believe how many men seek sexual relief with other women even though their first choice for a sex partner is the wife they already have.

They simply, mistakenly, believe that their wife really isn't very interested in it.

Why does this happen? Well, mainly, and almost unbelievably, through simple shyness, and the fear of rejection.

No matter how long they have been together, a man will still feel a sense of rejection if he begins to approach his wife with a large erection and loving in mind, and she turns around to him and says, "Not now, dear, I've got a headache/early start tomorrow/period/computer printout to analyze."

And no matter how long she has been having sexual relations with men, a woman will still feel that it is a man's job to make the first move in bed and that there is something embarrassing and even degrading about a woman showing just how hot she is to ball.

Many women are also concerned about showing sexual ignorance or incompetence. "I didn't like to take hold of his penis because I thought I might hurt him or hold it wrong and just not do anything for him."

You couldn't count the number of married couples who will lie in bed together tonight, each of them desperately feeling like physical loving, yet each of them too reticent for their own different reasons to do something about it.

There are some very quick and positive steps that any woman can take to show the man in her life that she is sexually active and sexually interested —steps that won't expose any sexual amateurishness and will encourage him to make love to her more frequently and more excitingly.

I won't pretend that taking these steps doesn't require *some* nerve on your part, but they are patterned on a tried-and-tested technique that has worked infallibly on men for countless centuries. You could call it the "You're-So-Strong-and-Clever-and-I'm-Just-a-Helpless-Woman Technique." You can see it in action by any roadside: a woman biting her lips and staring helplessly at a flat tire while a total stranger gets grease all over his new suit, changing the tire for her.

There's nothing demeaning about using this technique, because at the end of the transaction, whether it's changing a flat or enjoying sexual intercourse, both of you will feel better, and to my mind the whole purpose of human relationships is for both parties to feel better.

What you do is this: you initiate a sexual situation by purchasing some erotic item—either a sex aid of some kind, or an erotic book or magazine (even this book will do, now you've already bought it), or some sexy piece of clothing. Then, you show it to the man in your life and ask his expert advice about it.

Given those circumstances, there isn't a heterosexual man in the world who won't be only too pleased to assist you. In fact, you won't even be able to imagine how delighted he's going to be, because you will have taken the responsibility for initiating sex, without in any way compromising his male sexual ego. You will, in fact, have enlarged it. His male sexual ego, I mean—but that, too.

The only hard part—the part that requires nerve —is acquiring the sexual item in the first place. But, as we've seen, many sexual items such as vibrators and clitoral stimulators can be purchased by very discreet plain-cover mail order (look inside the back pages of *Playboy* for advertising from sex-catalog companies).

Here are some suggestions, ranging from the romantic to the raunchy, all based on the latest available lists, complete with genuine manufacturers' descriptions:

Nipple Delight Fluid   Nipple-lickin' delicous. Smear on to your partner's nipples, then slowly and tenderly lick it off "until she can't stand no more"—in strawberry, grape, or chocolate flavors.

Lotion d'Amour   Blow on it, it actually gets hot! Apply to any erogenous zone of your body and get your partner to blow on it. The sensuality is almost unbearable. Hot cinnamon, wild cherry, strawberry Margarita, fresh blueberry, Irish crème liqueur, piña colada and rum, or Swiss chocolate flavors.

Chocolate Dildo   Have you ever wanted to screw it, then chew it? Now's your chance with this slightly larger-than-life dildo in finest Swiss chocolate.

Kandi Condoms   May be worn by the male and licked off by the female, in delicious chocolate flavor.

Delay Spray   Is he too fast on the draw? This will slow him down! Contains a local anaesthetic so it really works. He'll surprise both you and him with his persistence—hope you can handle it!

Intimate Sexual Lubricant   Smooth and highly viscous fluid that helps to alleviate intimate friction.

Penis Heat Development Spray   So now he's too slow and flaccid. Never fear, this spray warms up and expands the penis to peak performance. "Please release me, let me go!"

Phemerone, the Lady Killer   If you'd like him to turn you on, then spray him with this. This is Phemerone, a concentrated form of female attractant that appeals to your subliminal senses so that he turns you on without you even realizing why.

Happy Ending   A soft brushlike vinyl stimulator worn around the base of the erect penis. Slip on while flaccid, and this super-quality restrictive device enhances the hardness of the penis. The device may be fitted at any angle to pleasure the female organ by stimulating the clitoris or the vaginal area.

Lustfingers   Bobbled vinyl finger sleeves to coax a woman into maximum receptivity, one vagina, one anal.

Penisator   A battery-operated ring that fits around the base of the penis and actually makes it vibrate while you're making love! Stimulates both the testicles and the vagina during intercourse. The vibrations can be controlled from gentle to superstrong.

Love Egg   A smooth plastic egg for insertion deep into the vagina ... It vibrates electrically while you sit back and enjoy its pleaures.

Once the items of your choice have arrived through the mail, how do you go about using them to your own best sexual advantage? Here's Carole, twenty-eight, a homemaker from Queens, New York, married for three years to Ted, thirty-one, an electrician for a construction corporation.

"We'd decided that we wouldn't have children for at least five years, so that we could have fun together while we were still young. But, I don't know, after the first year there didn't seem to be much fun in our marriage at all. There didn't seem to be much point to it, do you understand what I mean? It was just Ted getting up and eating breakfast and going off to work, and me sitting around the house all day watching TV. Then it was Ted coming home totally bushed, eating his evening meal, drinking a six-pack, and falling asleep.

"The only time we ever made love—I mean, really made love, not just a quick fuck—was on Sunday mornings. And after about a year of that, even *that* started to seem pretty routine, too. I mean, I always knew that as soon as Ted woke up on Sunday morning he'd reach over and start sticking his fingers up my pussy. He never satisfied me. Well, hardly ever. I started to believe that I didn't love him anymore. In fact, sometimes I started to believe I hated him. When he was away at work, I used to have fantasies about being seduced by Adam Carrington, you know, from *Dynasty*, and masturbating myself.

"It got to the point where I was masturbating two or three times a day, because I was so bored and lonesome and frustrated. I used to walk around the house with my hand in my panties all the time, diddling myself. My whole sex life was just a fantasy, it didn't include Ted anymore—well, hardly.

"About eighteen months after we were married a new girl called Margot moved in next door but one. She's real pretty and bright, and she was friendly right from the very first time we met. After I'd known her about two or three weeks, she caught me when I was feeling real depressed, and gradually I told her about me and Ted, about how bad our sex life was, and how there didn't seem to be any future in our marriage anymore.

"She said that her husband, Phil, had been married before, and that he'd had the same kind of marriage as me. I said, 'Well, that's not exactly encouraging, is it?' But she said that I shouldn't blame Ted, he probably didn't understand the way

I felt about sex; he probably didn't know what to do about sex. She said that Phil used to drink in the evenings, too, when he was married to his first wife. It was a way of copping out of the responsibility of making love to her.

"After the first couple of months of their affair, when they'd been balling every chance they got, Phil had moved in with her, and after a couple of weeks he was slipping into the same routine with her. Coming home tired, knocking back two or three martinis, falling asleep in the armchair. She said she waited for him to make love to her, but he didn't, no more than once or twice a week, and that was if she was lucky. She was beginning to think that she'd made a terrible mistake.

"But one day she had to meet a friend of hers at a big hotel, and her friend was late, so she took a look around the hotel pharmacy, and what did she see but a vibrator. She had half an idea that she was going to take it home to masturbate with it, the same way that I was always masturbating, but she bought it anyway. She said she was incredibly embarrassed, buying it, but the girl behind the counter didn't say anything at all, like it was totally normal.

"She took the vibrator home and she tried it. Well, I'd never seen one before, so I asked her what it was like. She went back to her house and she brought it around. It was just a plain one, white plastic, but it really buzzed when I switched it on. Margot lifted up her skirt and tugged down her panties—she wasn't at all embarrassed—and she showed me how she pressed the tip of the vibrator against her pubic hair, just above her clitoris, so that it vibrated her clitoris without actually touching it. Then she showed me how she ran the tip of it down the sides of her pussy, in between her outer lips and her inner lips, and when she was getting excited and juicy, how she'd slip it up inside her pussy and kind of stir it around and around.

"She asked me if I minded if she showed me how. Well, I didn't know what to say about that at first. I thought maybe she could be lesbian or something. But she was staightforward about it, you know? She was totally genuine. And she didn't try to kiss me or anything like that. So, in the end, I lifted up my skirt and let her do it.

"She told me to lie back on the couch and relax. Relax! She had to be kidding. But I tried my best. She lifted my knees a little, like this, and spread my pussy open with her fingers. I'd never been touched by a woman before, not like that, and it was the strangest sensation, but I can't say that I didn't like it. I mean, she touched me like she understood how I felt inside, and a man never does that.

"She pressed the tip of the vibrator very gently against my pubic hair. I didn't like the feeling of it at first and I thought it buzzed too loudly. But after a while my clitoris began to feel tingling and hot, the same way your legs feel when you've been running in the cold, and you suddenly come into the warm.

"I was still quite dry—nerves, I guess—but Margot took the vibrator away for a moment and pushed it right up inside her own pussy, 'for lubrication.' Then she opened the lips of my pussy even wider and slowly slid the vibrator up inside me, until it was deep inside and touching the neck of my womb and making my whole womb vibrate. At the same time Margot caressed my clitoris and very gently tugged at my pussy lips and rolled them between her fingers. I started to have sexual feelings like I'd never had before, ever. I suddenly saw what sex was all about: it was like this incredible feeling was tightening me up and tightening me up, and it didn't matter how blatant I was about it, when you feel like that, there isn't any such thing as being blatant or vulgar or whorish. The usual rules just don't apply.

"I lifted my hips because I wanted more and more, and I stretched open my pussy with my own fingers, right in front of this woman I hardly knew.

I began to feel like I was going to reach an orgasm when she took the vibrator out.

"I said, 'What are you doing, what? I was almost there!' But she said, 'There's more, this is the way to finish.'

"Well, the vibrator was real slippery now, and she pressed the tip of it against my anus. I said, 'No, not that.' I didn't like the idea of that at all, and besides, I was embarrassed because I thought it would be dirty. But Margot held the cheeks of my bottom wide open, and she pushed that vibrator right into me, right up to the very hilt, until I could feel her fingers caressing my stretched-open anus, caressing around and around, and all the time that deep buzzing feeling right up inside me.

"She reached for two cushions and tucked them under my bottom, another under my head, so that I could watch. She was driving me almost crazy by then, the way she was making me feel. I looked down between my legs and there was just the white butt of this vibrator sticking out from my bottom, and my anus fiery red, and my pussy wetter and shinier than I'd ever seen it before.

"I said, 'I'm there, I'm almost there,' but Margot said, 'No you're not.' She slipped one finger into my pussy, then two fingers, to open it up more, then three fingers. Then she tucked in her thumb and she slowly pushed her entire hand into my pussy, right up to the wrist. She worked it in and out, in and out, until it was good and slippery, and then right inside me she took hold of that buzzing vibrator that was up inside my bottom, and she gently massaged my pussy lining all around it, sliding it up and down with all four fingers.

"I don't have to tell you I had an orgasm that almost cracked me in half. I think I screamed out loud. But it went on and on, and when it was over, I lay there literally sobbing.

"Margot and I took a shower together, and she washed me, but she isn't a lesbian and she didn't treat me like one. She touched me sexually like any woman can touch any other woman sexually, to make her feel pleasure, without being in love with her, or committed to her—without being anything at all, but just a friend.

"We had coffee afterward, and we talked. Margot said that when she had first brought the vibrator home, she had pretty much done to herself what she had just done to me, and it was an eye-opener. Not because she preferred the vibrator to Phil's cock—she didn't; in fact, she didn't really care for the vibrator too much. But it had showed her what sex was like when you did it slowly, when you lavished care on it, and what she had wanted to do was to show that to Phil, too, because then they could both share the same feelings together.

"The trouble was, she said, that Phil was pretty macho, in his way, and she didn't think that he would have appreciated her giving him an exhibition of her masturbating with a vibrator, right in front of him. She had to do it in a way that made him feel good, like he was showing her.

"Well, what she did was to put it back in its carton—she even took out the batteries—and when Phil came home, she showed it to him. She told him the truth, that she had bought it in the hotel pharmacy while she was waiting for her friend. But she told a little white lie by saying that she had bought it quite innocently, as a massager. After all, that was what it said on the carton, Female Massage Kit. She said that she had shown her friend and that her friend had laughed and explained what it really was.

"She told him, 'It sounds pretty exciting. But how do you think it works?'

"After that, she said, she had him eating out of her hand. Usually he came home from work and all he wanted was a large martini. But this time she had him searching for batteries. He fitted them into the vibrator and showed her how it buzzed, and explained how it worked because it had a little odd weight in it that whizzed around and around. 'And then the woman just—'

"Well, Margot said, 'The woman just what? Show me. I'd love to know!'

"Phil took her into the bedroom, and undressed her, and kissed her, and showed her. At least that was what he thought he was doing, but all the time she was showing him. Both of them got really turned on, and by the time they were finished, the vibrator had disappeared into the bedclothes somewhere, but Phil and Margot were really making out.

"I wasn't sure how I was going to do the same thing with Ted. In fact, I was quite nervous about it. I thought he might take it all the wrong way and think that I was trying to suggest that his penis wasn't enough for me, or something like that. I was guilty about masturbating, too, and although I didn't feel guilty about what Margot and I had done together, it was the first sex that I had had with somebody else since Ted and I had gotten married. I don't think I felt as if I'd cheated on him or anything, but I didn't feel completely easy about it.

"Anyway, I bought a vibrator in a discount drugstore six or seven blocks away from where I usually shop. I didn't show it to Ted the first evening after I'd bought it, but I told him that I was suffering from a stiff neck, maybe from sleeping in a funny way, and could he massage it for me. Well, he did, and it was good, as a matter of fact, but I said that it still hurt some and that I was planning on going to the drugstore to buy something for it, maybe some embrocation.

"The next night I left the vibrator and a tube of embrocation on my dressing table. When Ted went into the bedroom to change, he called out, 'What the hell's this?' I said I'd bought it to massage my neck, and I blushed like crazy, I didn't even have to fake it. He said, 'Do you know what this is for? It's a vibrator!'

"I still played innocent. 'For sex,' he said. 'Don't

you understand?' He held it in front of his pants and said, 'Look! Remind you of anything?'

"It worked like a dream, because we both laughed about it like crazy. He thought that I was completely innocent, and so when I asked him to show me how it worked, he felt like he was being the expert.

"He didn't have Margot's gentle touch, but he had his own touch, which did a whole lot more for me than Margot's had, because he was my husband and I loved him. He undressed me, and he used the vibrator to massage my breasts, touching my nipples with the tip of it, so that they really stood out. Then he ran it all the way down my back and around my thighs. I mean, he used it like a real massager, and it felt sexy and good. I let him know that I liked it, too. Margot had told me how important that was. You have to murmur and wriggle around a little and close your eyes, even when you don't mean it, because after a while you'll get to mean it.

"Ted buzzed that vibrator all around my pussy, and then he ran it up and down his own penis and between his balls. I never saw his penis so hard and so big. He lifted my legs over his shoulders, and he pushed himself right inside of me, and I said, 'This is what I've wanted.' And Ted didn't even know how much I meant it.

"He fucked me beautifully. It was over quickly, because we were both so excited, but then he dipped the vibrator back inside me and buzzed it some more, and I had about seven or eight small orgasms, one after the other. I had to beg him to stop. Then he got his hard-on back, and he fucked me again, and then about an hour later he fucked me a third time, and when his penis started to grow soft, while he was fucking me, he pushed the vibrator up inside my pussy, alongside his own penis, the two of them together, and he made himself hard again, and for me it was totally fantastic, just like being fucked by two penises at once.

"We scarcely ever use it now, although it still lives in the nightstand drawer. We don't need to use it, because Ted got his confidence back, and I learned not to be so shy, that a woman isn't a whore just because she wants sex. Especially when the person she feels like sex with is your own husband, legally married."

There are some women who are not particularly partial to sexual hardware like vibrators or dildos or clitoral stimulators, although you should be reassured that, once they have played their part in a relationship, gadgets like these almost always end up gathering dust in the bedroom drawer, along with the sexy videos and the pornographic magazines and the open-crotch panties.

Sexual aids have an important part to play in many sexual relationships, but the mainstays of any lasting sexual relationship must be mutual affection, mutual excitement, and mutual respect. In the context of such a relationship, a vibrator or a dildo—or whatever you feel like enjoying yourself with—can be just the catalyst you need to remind each other how much you turn each other on. It can remind either one of you of the need you have for loving and well-considered stimulation. It can remind either one of you that, when you got married, or when you chose to live together, you were devoting your bodies to each other as well as your taste in bottled water and your joint mortgage.

With the proviso that either of you can always say, "No, that's enough," your husband's penis belongs to you, just as your vagina belongs to him. That was always one of the conditions of your getting together, unless you specifically said different. That's why you should never feel afraid to reach across the bed and take hold of his penis and rub it and massage it as much as you want. That's why, in return, your vagina should always be open to the man who loves you.

What if you feel that a sexual aid like a vibrator or a lust finger or a chocolate dildo isn't going to appeal to the man in your life? What if you're far too reticent to buy one?

Here's Miriam, thirty-two, from Covina, California, who didn't have to do any special shopping to excite William, her husband of six years' standing.

"I guess our love life was pretty routine. I didn't know why, I thought maybe we'd just gotten too used to each other. I didn't think I was sexually unattractive. I could lose a few pounds, maybe, I have very big breasts, 40-D, and I'm only five-six. But he always said that he liked big breasts. I mean, I knew that for a fact, the way he used to ogle Dolly Parton on TV.

"But it seemed like there wasn't a spark. He was busy and I was busy. He's a divorce lawyer and I work for the welfare department, and believe me, that kind of work takes up a whole lot of your time. I mean, all of your life. But I still felt that there was something lacking. Like sexually lacking. We were friends, we were affectionate, we kissed and we cuddled, we went to the theater together, but—I don't know—it's still pretty hard to describe. I felt like I was William's Wife. That was it. Like William's House or William's BMW or William's Nike sneakers. Can you understand what I'm saying? I knew that he loved me, but I felt like one of his possessions, rather than a person in my own right.

"When William wanted to make love, we made love. But for me that was never enough. I don't think for him it was ever enough. But he was always kind of a stuffed shirt, that was the way he was brought up. He needed something to stop him in his tracks.

"God knows I tried. I always dressed smartly and sprayed myself with Giorgio and went to bed wearing a peach silk nightdress. That was romantic, sure. But that was the kind of wife that William expected. Most evenings I spent an hour in the bathroom, trying to look erotic for him, but then he'd bounce into bed, read legal affidavits for ten minutes, then buss me on the cheek, switch off the light, and fall asleep. 'I'm a successful young lawyer, here's my well-groomed BMW, and, oh yes, here's my well-groomed wife.'

"One weekend about six or seven months ago, he brought home a batch of pornographic videos that had something to do with one of his divorce cases. He had to watch them for the hearing. I think the wife was claiming that her husband's interest in pornography had ruined their sex life, something like that. She should have been so lucky. Anyway William and I watched these videos, three or four hours of licking and sucking and screwing and girls bouncing up and down and going oh-oh-oh.

"I guess they turned us on. We made love twice while we were watching them. But when they were all finished, he went back to being lawyerish and businesslike, even though I was still feeling mucho horny. I slipped my hands into his pajamas pants and asked him why he never licked my cunt, the way the guys in those videos always licked their women's cunts. I said why didn't he put down his legal papers just for ten minutes and lick my cunt. But he wouldn't; he said he was too busy, he had a whole goddamned case to get ready for nine o'clock the following morning. So that was it. I turned over and sulked; he went on reading his legal papers.

"Before he went to sleep, though, he snapped at me, 'You're the last person in the world who can complain about having her cunt licked. God, I might as well kiss Judge C——!'

"By the time I woke up the following morning, he'd already left for the office. We hadn't even had time to make up. But after my exercises and after my shower, I took a good long look at myself in the dressing-room mirror, and I thought, 'What's wrong here, Miriam? And what the hell does Judge C—— have to do with it?'

"The answer was so darned simple I couldn't help laughing. Judge C—— has a thick black mustache. And when I looked down at my cunt, what did I have? I've always had thick wavy black hair on my head, and I've always been proud of it, my crowning glory. But my pubic hair was just as shaggy and just as thick, and there I was, wondering why William wouldn't lick my cunt.

"I thought about it for a whole weekend. I thought, Michael loves me, I know that he loves me, but there is something he doesn't want to do. He doesn't want to have oral sex with me, not because he doesn't like the idea of oral sex, but because my cunt is too bushy.

"But somehow, you know, I've always been a very strong-willed independent woman, with a job of her own, and I thought to myself, Why should I compromise my natural appearance for the sake of titillating my husband? He knew what I was like when he married me, he took me for better or for worse. This is the way I am. I'm not a child with no pubic hair. I'm a grown woman.

"I have to admit it, I had a real mental fight about this. But in the end I made up my mind by accident. They had a sale in my favorite fashion store in Covina, and I went it to try on this really pretty sleeveless dress they had in the window. They have kind of a communal changing room for women in there, and when I went in, a very good-looking woman of about forty-one or forty-two was trying on a pair of slacks. She was wearing pantyhose but no panties, and I couldn't help noticing that she had no pubic hair at all—I mean, her vagina was completely bare.

"I plucked up as much courage as I could, and I asked her what depilatory she used. You know, for what they diplomatically call the bikini area. To my surprise she was quite open and unembarrassed about it. She said she used Louis Marcel wax, once or twice a week, and that was all she had to do. But she looked at me and said, 'Scissors first, and then a razor. Then the wax.'

"I asked her why she did it. She said because she preferred it. It was cleaner, and it was neater, and it looked better, and the last thing she said was that her husband liked her that way. She said that she had shaved her pubic hair ever since it first appeared, because her mother had always shaved hers, and she had always thought that it was the natural thing to do. Her mother had told her that men prefer it that way.

"I said it seemed like pandering to men's fantasies, to shave your cunt. But she said, 'It's no different from men shaving their chins, it's all vanity, and what's so terrible about a little vanity. Do it for yourself,' she said, 'not for him, and if he happens to like it, which he will, then all well and good.'

"I bought the dress. I don't know why. I guess I made a decision, that was all. After that, I went to the pharmacy and bought myself a razor. I felt as guilty as if I'd been buying condoms. I was sure the pharmacist was staring at me and thinking to himself, that woman is going to go home and shave her cunt. Isn't that ridiculous?

"When I got home, I thought about shaving myself immediately, so that I could surprise William when we went to bed that night. But then I thought, No . . . if I do that, I'm going to be just like one of those women who leaps into the bedroom wearing a black G-string and tassels on her tits, and says 'ta-rraaaa!' Don't get me wrong, there must be some women who do that and some husbands who like it, but Michael always likes to feel that he's in control. He's like a lot of men, especially with sex. They think that they're supposed to know everything about it, even when they don't. Nobody's ever told them that they're not expected to. Do you know, when I was seventeen, I had a boyfriend who took out his cock when he was just about to come and pressed it up against my navel. He thought that was what you were supposed to do.

"I left the razor beside the basin in the bathroom and I waited all evening until bedtime. William went in to take a shower, and he picked it up and said, 'This isn't for me? I only use electric.'

"I came into the bathroom and said, 'No, it's for

me, I bought some new swimsuits today, and I can't wear them without shaving, because they're so high-cut. I'm not very sure how to use it.' I was hoping that, the first time, he could show me how to do it.

"Can you believe it, my own husband, bless his heart, went all glassy-eyed and dry-throated? He said, 'Sure, sure, sure I'll show you. You mean you want to shave your ... ?' And I nodded, like I didn't know anything about anything.

"He took me through to the bedroom, and he undressed me so tenderly, it was just like our wedding night. When he took down my panties, he ran his hand through my pubic hair, tangling his fingers in it, and then he leaned over and smiled at me and kissed me.

"He used nail scissors first of all, cutting all the long hair off as short as he could. Then he ran me a bath, and I lay back in the bath while he soaped my cunt, and that felt delightful; he hadn't soaped me like that since the very first bath we took together, massaging my clitoris and slipping his soapy fingers up inside of me.

"After that, he put his left hand underneath my bottom and lifted me out of the water just a little, then he began to shave me, very carefully, all round my vagina, until I was completely bare.

"I hadn't seen my cunt bare like that since I was a little girl, but when I did, I kind of changed my mind about it. I guess I'd always been suspicious that men liked women to shave their cunts because they wanted them to look like children. But a woman's cunt isn't anything like a child's. It's very full, you know, like a kind of blossoming flower, with very intricate lips. And when you open it up, you can see your clitoris poking out like a bright-pink bud, and the tiny hole that you pee from, and then this moist glistening cunt hole; I can understand why men want to see it without any hair: it's fascinating, and it's beautiful, just like a man's cock is beautiful, it's not just a hidden slit behind some hair.

"We said hardly anything at all. William took me into the bedroom and stood me naked in front of the glass, and there I was, a small quite-pretty woman with dark wavy hair, and huge big-nippled breasts, and a rounded tummy, and a completely naked cunt. He sat on the edge of the bed behind me and drew me back on to his lap, and his cock was sticking up stiff and crimson, with huge swollen veins, and his balls were as hard and tight as golf balls.

"Very, very gently, he opened up my cunt with his fingers, and I watched him in the mirror as he lifted me up a little and pushed his cock right into me. It was incredible. It took only two or three strokes, and then he clutched me around the waist, so tight that I could hardly breathe, and I felt his come pumping up into me, I could truly feel it, one pump after another. It can't be any hotter than body temperature, can it, but somehow it felt hot.

"I thought then that William might have finished, because usually he turned over, after he'd come, and went immediately to sleep. But that night he lifted me up off his lap and laid me back on the bed, and when I asked him what he was doing, he simply shushed me.

"I lay back looking at the ceiling, and I felt his hands opening my thighs, then the warm wet tip of his tongue on my clitoris. I remember I said, 'Ohhhh!' That was all I could think of saying, but I remember thinking, He's licking my cunt, just like the men in those pornographic videos. He's doing what he said he couldn't do, he's doing it, and he's doing it to me.

"He ran his tongue all the way around my cunt, and then he pressed his lips right up against me and pushed his tongue up inside me as far as he could, and all I can say to any woman whose husband has never done that, it's out of this world. I lifted my head and looked down, and he was just lifting his head away from me, and there was sperm on his tongue, pearly-white streaks of his own sperm.

"I reached down and took hold of his head in my hands and drew him up to me and kissed him, so that I could taste the same sperm that he had, and my own juice, too. I swallowed it and swallowed it, and even though it tastes rather dry, after a while, quite astringent, I knew that I wanted more.

"I suppose it sounds like exaggeration, now, to say that my marriage changed that night. It wasn't so much what I did. It was the decision I made to get us both out of a sexual rut. I didn't want to shave myself, believe me. And vibrators? I wouldn't have bought a vibrator, not for anything. I always believed in feminine integrity. Not so much feminism as a revolutionary cause, but feminism as something to be respected and valued.

"But what can I tell you? I feel no less feminine for having no pubic hair. In fact, in a way, I feel more feminine, because I'm showing my husband that I'm a woman, I'm showing off my cunt, and my husband not only likes to look at it and fuck it, but he likes to kiss it and lick it, too. There can't be any feeling of feminism stronger than having a naked man kneeling between your thighs, with his cock sticking out and just about to burst, and his tongue right up your vagina. God, I sound like Miriam the Dominatrix, don't I? But it's not like that at all.

"I asked him to show me how to shave, and somehow he still thinks of it as his idea. He's always complimenting me these days, how sexy I am. How many wives can put their hands on their hearts and say that their husband compliments their cunt? 'You have a beautiful cunt,' when does he ever say that? But all women do have beautiful cunts. I lay in bed last night . . . Do you think this is getting too personal? I lay in bed last night, after William and I had made love, and I cupped my hand over my cunt and slipped my middle finger up inside, and I was filled to the brim with sperm. I left my finger up inside and thanked God for William, and thanked God for marriage, and thanked God for all those wonderful things that two people can do to show that they love each other."

So Miriam initiated a revival in her sex life by using nothing more spectacular than a razor. She was strong-willed and self-critical enough, however, to have identified one of the most obvious causes of her husband's disaffection, and to have taken steps to do something about it.

Doing something about it is critical. There are countless women who know what's wrong with their sex lives, or can hazard a pretty accurate guess, but who refuse to do anything about it. I'm not going to lower myself. It's up to the man. I'm not going to buy a vibrator. I'm not going to smear my breasts with peppermint-flavored glop. I'm not going to wear a G-string; only strippers wear G-strings. I'm not going to shave *my* pubic hair, thank you very much. It's vulgar, it's rude, it's whorish. If he really loved me, he wouldn't need anything like that. And he's certainly not going to touch my bottom, let him just try.

Women who react negatively to the idea of doing anything raunchy to arouse their men are failing to understand that all happy and exciting sexual relationships require commitment and enthusiasm from both partners.

Equally, men who fail to seduce their women romantically and emotionally, men who fail to take the trouble to create a warm and loving atmosphere and who come and go before their women are fully aroused—men like that deserve no more than they get.

One of the best ways in which you can induce your man to do something sexual for you is to buy a good sex manual, and then ask him to explain it you, preferably in practical terms.

Lydia, a twenty-six-year-old secretary from Detroit, wrote to me twice about her sexual difficulties with her husband, Paul. "It's not that he doesn't love me," she complained. "It's just that he hardly ever manages to turn me on. We make love the same way every time, with him on top and me underneath, and I've had only two climaxes since we first started sleeping together."

My suggestion to Lydia was that she should buy herself a copy of *How to Drive Your Man Wild in Bed* and invite Paul to join her in reading it and exploring its possibilities. Later, she wrote, "I read it myself first, then what opened my eyes more than anything was that what I used to think of as way-out sex is done by quite ordinary normal happy people. I wasn't told very much about sex when I was growing up, because my mother and father didn't get on too well, and all I ever heard about sex from my mother was that it was a kind of intrusion that women just had to endure.

"I knew that sex wasn't like that, or at least that it didn't have to be. The first boy I ever slept with, when I was sixteen, was quite a lot older than me, twenty-two, and he was experienced enough to make it pleasant and exciting, apart from taking proper precautions. But I still thought that oral sex and things like that were way-out and dirty, I guess, and as for sexy underwear and sex toys and doing it in the open air and tying people up, I certainly couldn't imagine myself doing anything like that.

"So, it was quite a surprise to find out that millions of couples enjoy oral sex, that it isn't wrong or dirty for a woman to suck her husband's penis or for a man to kiss his wife's vagina. It was also a surprise to find out that almost everybody has some kind of sex fantasy, because I always used to feel guilty about having sexy thoughts when Paul was making love to me. I used to have this particular fantasy that came from when I was young and I used to go to riding school, and it makes me blush now to write about it, but of course I know now that it's perfectly normal to think about 'dirty' things when you're making love.

"When I was at riding school I saw this big white stallion having an erection. I didn't think about it for years afterward, but one night we'd been out for dinner and had a few drinks, and Paul woke me up about two o'clock in the morning and started making love to me. While he was doing it, I had a fantasy that I was standing naked in the stables and that I was massaging this stallion's huge red erection, while at the same time Paul—at least it was Paul—was standing behind me and pressing his cock against my bare bottom and squeezing my breasts. I hope you don't mind my writing so frankly, but it's difficult to use any other kind of words.

"In this fantasy Paul slips his cock into my cunt and starts to make love to me standing up, and all the time I'm rubbing and massaging this horse's cock, too. In the end we're both wildly excited, and Paul comes inside me, and I give the stallion a last frantic rub, and it shoots huge squirts of warm sperm all over my stomach and my thighs. I remember one the stablehands at the riding school saying that stallions shot out bucketloads when they came, and I guess that word stuck in my subconscious.

"When I first had this fantasy, when Paul was making love to me that night, I had a climax. That was only the second climax I had ever had in our relationship. But I felt so dirty-minded afterward, you have no idea how embarrassed and ashamed I felt. I felt as bad as if I'd actually gone out and masturbated a real horse. When Paul had gone back to sleep, I lay in the dark and cried, because I felt that there must be something sexually wrong with me.

"Of course, what your book showed me was that everybody has so-called dirty fantasies and that they're nothing to be ashamed of; they're just things we think about to excite ourselves and to excite our lovers. After reading your book I allowed myself for the first time to think about that fantasy again, and even to go over it and over it, and enjoy it. I dared myself to think about the dirtiest things that I could, even sucking the stallion's cock and letting it shoot out all those bucketloads of sperm all over me, into my mouth, everything.

"I faced up to the fact that I had a sexual imagination and that it simply meant that I was a normal, sexually active woman. I faced up to my embarrassment and I faced up to my shame, and they melted away and I've never felt ashamed or embarrassed about my sexuality since.

"Then I was ready to include Paul in what I'd discovered. But, of course, I didn't want him to feel inadequate in any way. He's quite a sensitive man, and I knew that if I just gave him the book and said, 'Here, read this, and you might be a better lover,' well, he would take that all wrong, and probably I'd be doing a whole lot more damage to our relationship than good.

"So during the evening, when he was finishing off his accounts, I sat reading the book quite openly, and when I could see that he had almost finished, I came over to him and said, 'Is this true, do you think, that men like oral sex so much? Would you like it?'

"Well, he took the book and said, 'What the hell's this?'—not nastily, or anything, but just surprised. I said that one of my girlfriends at the office had lent it to me, because she'd just finished reading it and she said that it had made her a much better lover.

"I told him that I thought I was very inexperienced and that I was afraid of disappointing him in bed, and so I thought I ought to read it, too. The trouble was, I wasn't sure about most of it, whether men really liked having their cocks sucked so much, and what they liked a woman to do to turn them on.

"I have to tell you that I had him hooked then. I think everybody gets hooked when you start to talk about sex, because it's a subject that everybody's interested in, but they never usually get the chance to discuss it. They've always got thousands of questions, even about the simplest things. And the one thing a man always seems to want to know from a woman, and a woman seems to want to know from a man, is What does it feel like when I do that to you? Because I think quite often things that turn a man on don't particularly turn a woman on, and vice versa.

"Anyway the result of my bringing *How to Drive Your Man Wild in Bed* home was pretty good. Paul practically snatched it from me and started reading aloud and making comments, like 'Yes, I'd really like it if you did that,' or 'No, I wouldn't like that too much.'

"In the end I said, 'Let's take the book to bed with us and try it.' So we did. I told him I wanted to start with the part about oral sex, because even though I'd kissed his cock once or twice, I'd always been afraid to put it into my mouth or suck it or anything in case he didn't like it or I hurt him, or in case I did it wrong and he just found it boring and off-putting and the whole thing just went flat.

"So Paul lay back and read the book out loud, and I followed the instructions, and I have to tell you we had the best time, friendly and funny but very, very sexy!

"He read out the bit on page seventy-four that says 'You can give his penis a few gentle sucks, and you'll probably need to when your mouth fills with saliva and the few drops of lubricant juice that emerge from the end of his cock. But most of the time you should be drawing the glans in and out of your mouth, caressing it with your lips, and using your tongue to probe the tiny opening, the frenum, and the corona.'

"Paul was incredibly hard, his cock was enormous, and I started to think about my stallion fantasy. What with that and Paul reading out all your sexual instructions to me, I began to feel as if I was burning up, I was so turned on. I put one hand down between my legs and started to masturbate myself while I was sucking him, I simply had to. I'd never done that before; Paul could see what I was doing, but it only turned him on even more. His head of his cock flew in and out of my mouth, really quickly and lightly, just like you suggest in the book, and at the same time I was rubbing the shaft of it, harder and harder.

"He got to the part where the book asks, 'Should you swallow the man's sperm or not?' and I didn't even get the chance to decide. Paul just shot off into my mouth, the first squirt went straight down my throat, the rest of it all over my lips. At the same time I climaxed too, and I collapsed on top of him feeling as if the whole ceiling had come down.

"Our sex life is so much better now. It's not perfect. I don't think anybody's sex life is perfect. But at least it's much more exciting and we do different things. There's no shame in admitting that a book can help you. Sometimes the problem is not so much that you don't know the facts of life. It's thinking that you're sexually peculiar for wanting to make love so much or for wanting your husband to do certain things to you. A book also helps in that you can show it your husband so that he can learn what you want out of your sex life without you having to tell him to his face that he's not satisfying you properly.

"Finding out that I was sexually normal and that it's quite healthy to enjoy sex and that just because you have fantasies about stallions and orgies and sucking men's penises and things like that, you're not sick or dirty or anything—that to me was the most liberating thing ever."

7

Affairs of the Heart

Some women appear to have the ability to attract men without even trying. You've noticed them at every party, at every social gathering. They may not be particularly pretty. They may not even have the kind of figure that would usually turn heads. But men cluster around them like moths around a kerosene lamp, flattering them, flirting with them, and treating them like stars.

You may not particularly wish to be that kind of a woman. You may prefer a quieter, more predictable existence and a much more stable relationship with the man or men in your life. But haven't you ever wondered what qualities a woman like that possesses to make her so alluring to men? And wouldn't you like to possess just a few of those qualities, even if you use them on your own man, and nobody else?

If you take a look at women who magnetically attract men, you will notice that they mostly have several clearly identifiable qualities. You can cultivate those qualities in yourself to make yourself more attractive to men generally—and more attractive to your husband or lover in particular.

You will also be able to compete with any woman your husband or lover happens to meet, no matter how much she flutters her eyelashes at him, because he will always be sure that he can get better from you.

There is, of course, no absolute certainty in sexual relationships. Passions grow and passions sometimes fade. Quite often there comes a time when you simply don't want a relationship to continue. But there is a great deal you can do to make sure that any relationship that you *want* to last, lasts.

One of the most important qualities of all is confidence. Confidence in yourself, confidence in your ability to attract and excite the man in your life. Confidence that you can keep his attention on you, no matter where he goes or what his chances are of meeting another attractive woman.

Having this kind of confidence is nothing to do with being overassertive or loud or bossy or even particularly flirtatious. We're talking about the quiet confidence of knowing what you are, knowing what your personal value is, and of being better in bed than any woman you can think of. What has Liz Taylor got that you haven't got? Do you think that Bo Derek is any better in bed than you are? Could Daryl Hannah satisfy your man as well as you?

You know what the answers are. Nothing, no, and no. You are an attractive woman. You're not lacking in any way at all . . . except that you don't assert yourself with the man in your life and haven't done enough to exploit your natural potential.

How do I know that you haven't done enough to exploit your natural potential?

Because very few women have, even those other women who have men clustering around them. Sexually, every woman has much more going for her than she believes, both physically and mentally.

It's difficult to discover just how much better a lover you could be, particularly if you have no ready access to sexual literature and movies, and particularly if the man in your life keeps telling you that he's quite satisfied with you the way you are. He may well be satisfied, because he doesn't know any better. But what's going to happen if he meets a woman who has such a sparkling array of sexual talents that you suddenly look like last year's model?

I've written this to women again and again. Don't

judge your sexual potential by your partner's apparent satisfaction with the way things are. Always strive to be more exciting, always be prepared to try new techniques, always keep one step ahead of the game. That way, the chances that your man will ever grow tired of you will be minimal.

You'll find plenty of new suggestions in this book for improving your love life and widening your sexual horizons. But confidence begins not with a new sexual act, but with you yourself.

The very best way to start improving your sexual confidence is to take a good long look at yourself in the mirror. Are you happy with what you see? It might be the middle of the day and you might be dressed in pretty ordinary around-the-house clothes, but are you still well-groomed and appealing? Is your hair washed, well-styled? Are you wearing any cosmetics? Perfume? How about your nails?

Ask yourself this: If a gorgeous new man walked into your life right now, do you think that he'd find you attractive, the way you are, right this minute?

If you can truthfully answer "yes" to that question, if you feel well-dressed and happy to face up to anyone, then you've already made a very important start in becoming sexually self-confident.

Here's Adeline, a forty-four-year-old beautician from Palm Springs, California: "My mother was a beautician before me, and she taught me right from the very beginning that a woman should spend twenty minutes on herself every single morning before she does a stroke of work. If you can't find twenty minutes to spend on yourself every morning, you should set your alarm twenty minutes earlier. Don't ever think of doing anything, not even driving the children to school, unless you've spent that time on yourself.

"My mother didn't believe that it was sexually demeaning for a woman to make herself look good. She thought that men ought to make themselves look good, too. She certainly wouldn't have approved of designer stubble and unwashed hair. She always said that grooming was a matter of respect for others and respect for yourself. And she wore scarcely any makeup. She didn't believe in thick layers of foundation or bright-red lipstick, even when they were fashionable.

"She simply believed in keeping your hair clean and tidy, your skin clean and well-toned-up, your nails trimmed, and all your superfluous hair waxed. Nice smooth legs, nice smooth underarms.

"If you always make sure that your clothes are bright and fresh and well-pressed, you'll have ten times more confidence with everyone around you. And, of course, that includes men.

"One thing she always used to nag me about was underwear. She used to say that the trouble with most women was that they didn't throw their underwear away when they should. She was always buying herself new bras and new stockings and new pantyhose and throwing away the old ones. It was interesting, though, that she wore stockings and a garter belt, but she hardly ever wore panties, and I don't either, and neither does my daughter. She always used to say that panties were unnecessary, and in any case she always used to feel more feminine without them. If women do wear panties, though, they should replace them regularly, so that they never feel as if they're wearing something that they wouldn't like a man to see them in. I guess you've heard the old caution: always wear your good underwear when you go out, in case you get knocked down a bus. Well, it's not a bad caution. You might meet the man of your dreams, and how are you going to feel if you're wearing a pair of panties that are fit for nothing but cleaning the silver with?"

Many women lack sexual confidence when it comes to their naked bodies. They look at themselves in the mirror and they simply hate their breasts—too big, too small, too flat, too floppy. They hate their waistlines. They hate their thighs.

My advice to any woman who feels that there is

anything wrong with the way she looks in the nude is to go out and buy herself a couple of copies of *Playboy* or *Penthouse* or *Hustler.* I worked for ten years as a senior editor for *Penthouse* and I saw literally hundreds of women naked. The variation in their figures was remarkable. And what was also remarkable was that it wasn't their bodies that made the sexy ones sexy. Some of the girls whose photographs drew the most enthusiastic response from readers were short and dumpy, or thin and small-breasted.

What made them sexy was the way in which they presented their nudity. Self-confidently, proudly, happy, and pleased with themselves. They enjoyed showing their naked bodies off.

I'm not suggesting that you show yourself off to anybody except that special man in your life, let alone the millions of readers of men's magazines. But if you show pleasure and joy in displaying your body to your husband or lover, that pleasure and joy will be reflected in his greater appreciation of you.

Jacquie, a thirty-one-year-old music teacher from Denver, Colorado, wrote to me asking for advice on whether she should go for cosmetic surgery on her breasts, and also if I could recommend exercises that would trim her stomach. She said that she felt embarrassed about her figure and she always made sure she wore loose and shapeless clothes, and that she never undressed in front of her husband because she thought she looked like "a whale." She said that her sex life was "not at all active" and that she had seen the way her husband looked at other, thinner women, and felt "to be candid about it, incipient panic." She sent me a Polaroid picture of herself wearing nothing but a small pair of transparent panties.

Jacquie was very large-breasted, and in common with many women who have a fuller figure, her hips were generous and her stomach was rounded. But it was quite obvious why her husband had been attracted to her. She had a very pretty face, dark curly hair, and big blue eyes. Even though the size of her breasts made it difficult for her to find fashionable dresses to fit ("The top buttons always burst open," she complained), and the roundness of her stomach made it hard for her to find comfortable and good-looking skirts and slacks, she was far more sexually attractive than she realized, and it was her self-image that was the principal obstacle to her dressing well.

Her self-image was also the principal difficulty in her sex life.

She was a pretty and accomplished woman with a truly stunning figure, and the potential to be even more stunning. But she just couldn't see herself that way.

The first thing I did was to pay Jacquie the compliments she deserved. Nobody looks their best in a self-taken Polaroid, but I could tell that she was quite gorgeous, and I told her so. The next thing I did was to make some practical suggestions, and those practical suggestions were based on the real experiences of women who managed to turn their sex lives right around, from physical and emotional disaster to pleasure and satisfaction.

Jacquie had to look at her grooming. Her hair was luxuriant, but needed expert and regular cutting. She had to think about her nails and her eyebrows and smoothing her legs, and all the other details of personal feminine attention that she had let slip, simply because she thought she was so unattractive.

There were some simple nonstrenuous exercises that Jacquie could do to trim her stomach. I usually recommend The Curl, which you can find described in Time-Life's excellent book *Getting Trim*. She needed to diet a little, too. Nothing too drastic, but sexual unhappiness and frustration often leads to women eating more than they should, particularly "comfort" foods like cookies and candies. The result: more weight and even more unhappiness.

The single most important thing that Jacquie had

to do, however, was to start believing that she was sexy.

Many women with exceptionally large breasts find the goggle-eyed attention they get from men to be most unwelcome. Jacquie was the same. But I encouraged her to think of her body with pride, not with shame, and to see that the problem lay not with her, but with the crudeness and insensitivity of the men who responded so blatantly.

Most of all, I encouraged her to be proud of her body in front of her husband. He must have been attracted to her to marry her in the first place. By covering herself up and behaving as if she were ashamed of her looks, she was making him feel as if she didn't enjoy having sex with him, as if there were something wrong with their relationship, and perhaps worst of all, she was making him feel that perhaps he had poor taste in women.

How often have I heard women saying to their lovers, "I don't know what you see in me." How often have I heard women responding to a compliment by saying, "Don't be ridiculous, I'm not beautiful."

I know why women do it. They do it because they're shy and because they're lacking in self-confidence and they don't know how to take a compliment. If they learned to accept that their husbands just happen to love them for what they are, and that sometimes they just happen to feel like expressing that love by telling them how beautiful and sexy they find them, then their husbands would feel a whole lot more satisfied and more content. They might even begin to feel that they did make the right choice of wife, after all.

The more compliments you rebuff, the fewer you'll get. So, why not accept them with a smile (and a blush, if they make you blush) and a simple thank-you. That's all it takes. And, believe me, you'll get more. You deserve them, after all.

Here's what happened to Jacquie, in her own words: "I was very encouraged by your reply. I had begun to feel deeply depressed about myself and about my marriage, and I was sure that it wouldn't be long before Mike found somebody thinner and sexier and more attractive than me. In fact, I was almost willing it to happen so that I could get it all over with.

"You have made me feel like an attractive woman again. I know that I was letting myself go, not worrying about my appearance and being generally moody and difficult to live with. But I decided all that was behind me. I was going to be proud of myself.

"My confidence was shaken again by taking a close look in the mirror, but I went out and had my hair cut and tinted, and I had a manicure at the same time. Also I went looking for clothes that showed my body off rather than hiding it, and you would be quite amazed how many clothes I found that suited my figure. I found a beautiful black button-through dress with revers lapels that actually showed off my cleavage!

"The hardest thing to do was to show myself off to Mike. For a woman who's used to her husband seeing her naked, this must sound ridiculous. But I had reached a point where I always made sure that I put on a towel or a wrap so that Mike wouldn't look at me. You suggested that I should spend a whole day at home completely naked and that I should still be naked when Mike came back. Well, I did it, and I felt very strange and nervous.

"But I did the other things you suggested, too, which was to take a warm bath early in the afternoon and spend some time with a mirror, touching myself and examining myself sexually. You are quite right that when you take a good long look at your own vagina, you can see the beauty in it, and see what it is that men find attractive about it. I masturbated, too, until my vaginal juice began to flow, although I didn't masturbate completely to orgasm. I admit that I was very hesitant to taste my own vaginal juice, but it is practically tasteless, if slightly sweet, and certainly not repellent.

"I could not think how Mike was going to react when I opened the door for him naked. Well, when he came home, he was quite surprised, to say the least, and asked me if he'd caught me halfway through a shower. I hugged him and I kissed him, and I told him the truth: that I'd allowed the sexual side of me to hibernate lately, but that now I'd decided that everything was going to be different.

"I took off his coat and loosened his necktie and unbuttoned his shirt. He did most of the rest of his undressing all by himself. I told him to lie back on the couch and close his eyes, and I'd make him feel good. I knelt beside him, and his cock was sticking up so hard that it almost reached his belly button. I took his cock in my hand, and for the very first time in my life I licked it. It tasted salty and strong, but I wanted more of it. I pressed my lips against it and then I opened up my mouth and took the whole plum into my mouth.

"I sucked him and licked him and ran my tongue tip all the way down the shaft of his cock and between his balls. He didn't say a word, not a single word, but he shivered. Once I'd actually plucked up the courage to take his cock into my mouth, I didn't want to stop. I wanted to chew it and swallow it. I suddenly realized the joy of what you'd said: that I was Mike's wife and I could do anything I wanted with his cock, it was mine just as much as it was his.

"And to think I'd been so embarrassed about showing myself! I looked up and saw myself in the mirror on the other side of the room, a naked woman kneeling beside a man, with her cheek bulging out because her mouth was cramful of hard cock, and I don't think that I'd ever seen anything so intimate or erotic or beautiful in my whole life.

"I ran my tongue around and around his cock and squashed it up against my lips and kissed it and buried it in my cleavage, so that he was fucking my two big breasts, in and out, in and out, just like fucking my vagina. My cleavage was slippery with his cock juice, and I think I would have been quite happy to let him climax between my breasts, if you hadn't insisted that I shouldn't hurry, that I should do everything I felt like.

"I climbed on top of him and I guided his cock up into my vagina with my hand. Then I very slowly made love to him, at my own pace. You said I should make sure to have intercourse at my own pace. Mike kissed my nipples and pressed his face into my breasts, and I could see how much he adored my breasts, and all the time I'd been thinking that they were far too big and that he hated them as much as I did. Well, I didn't any longer.

"Mike came very suddenly. One moment I was sliding up and down, the next he was shooting right up inside of me. I waited for just a moment, but I wanted more, I wanted him to satisfy me. So I knelt over his face and opened my vagina wide with my fingers.

"Remember that I'd never done anything like that before, so for me this was quite an emotional and sexual achievement. I'd never let Mike look at my vagina, not in the sense that I'd ever given him the opportunity to examine it; I'd always assumed that my vagina wasn't the kind of thing that a man would want to look at. But he looked at it now, and he lifted his head up and kissed me, right between my vaginal lips, even though I was still wet from fucking. Then his own sperm dripped out of me, on to his chin and his neck and his mouth, but he didn't care at all. He started to lick me with his tongue, all around my vagina, and then he started to lick my clitoris, very quickly.

"Occasionally he licked me a little too hard. But then I'd lift myself up a little, almost out of his reach, and he'd take the hint. But most of the time it was marvelous. He licked quicker and quicker, just the very tip of his tongue butterfly-kissing my clitoris—on and on, until I truly didn't know where

I was. With his hands he squeezed and massaged my thighs—those thighs of mine, which I'd always considered so fat and unattractive—and then he pulled open the cheeks of my bottom, lubricated his fingertip with sperm and vaginal juice mixed together, and ran it around and around my anus, occasionally just slipping the very tip of his finger inside my ass.

"I almost collapsed when I came. It was one of the best ever. And what made it even better was that I felt sexy again. I felt proud of myself. We lay together on the couch cuddling each other and kissing and talking, and then after a while Mike said, 'That was brilliant, you can get dressed now.' But I said no. There wasn't any need for me to dress, I was going to stay naked.

"We had the sexiest night you can ever imagine. I did things that night that I've only ever dreamed about, or read about. I lost all of my sexual inhibition and showed Mike that I was proud of myself, proud of my body, and that I loved him. It changed my life, and that is no exaggeration.

"If you ever publish this, and any of your women readers think that it can't be true, that your sex life can change so dramatically in just a single night, then I wish that you could publish this picture of Mike and me that we took that same evening. These days, I'm glowing with self-confidence, everybody says how much more attractive I look (and slimmer, too!), and I still get those wolf whistles and those men with the bulging eyes. However, I simply don't care because I'm happy."

The new Polaroid that Jacquie sent shows a very pretty woman with shining highlighted curls. She has her eyes closed, but she is obviously acutely aware of what she is doing. In her fists she is clenching an erect penis—about a quarter of an inch away from her partly opened mouth. She is clenching the penis so tight that its head is swollen and dark purple. The camera's flash has caught a jet of thick white sperm flying from the penis and touching the woman's front teeth. The tip of her tongue has just emerged to catch it.

A woman who can send me such a photograph—and sent it with such pride—is a woman who has discovered the full excitement that sex can offer her. Not sex with a different partner every night, however—not dangerous sex or illegal sex or perverted sex. But simply the sex that a man and a woman can find together within their own existing relationship, no matter how long that relationship has been going on or how hopeless is may seem to be.

Somebody has to make the first move, and as we have seen again and again, this first move is usually more effective if it is taken by you, the woman. If you have enough confidence in yourself, if you believe in your own sexual attractiveness, if you can lay aside your caution and your embarrassment, then your marriage can give you sexual rewards that you never even dreamed of.

One of the expectations that many women have about sex is that, somehow, every single sexual act is going to be mutually satisfying. In almost every romantic novel you read, the hero and the heroine manage to climax together and then both lie back sated and blissful and equally satisfied.

This concept of sex is both erroneous and damaging. While mutual climaxes are highly exciting, it isn't even realistic to attempt to reach simultaneous orgasm, or to think of it as any kind of sexual ideal. In fact, the most satisfied lovers are almost always those who take it in turns.

Not only is it unrealistic to strive for mutual climaxes, it is also unrealistic to think that no sex can take place between you if one or other of you doesn't happen to feel like it. Suppose you don't actually feel like having intercourse. There is still no reason why you shouldn't caress and play with your man and bring him to a climax with your fingers. Similarly, even if he doesn't feel too much like it, he can still caress you sexually.

This is Marcia, twenty-seven, a lawyer's receptionist from Chicago. Her husband, Andy, six years her senior, was married before, and divorced. Marcia said, "If you ask me what my technique is, for getting and keeping a man, it's never saying no. Too many women say no too often, then they wonder why their husbands up and leave them. My experience is that men can want sex just like that, *paff!* at the drop of a hat. The urge just hits them and they want it, and they're all ready for it, too, with their dicks sticking out like coat pegs, and they get so frustrated if the woman in their life says, 'Zipper up that coat-peg and forget it. You may feel like rutting like a bull, but I sure don't. I've got all this ironing to do.'

"My moral is, forget about the ironing. The ironing can wait ten minutes. When I first went out with Andy, he was amazed that I didn't mind where he fucked me or when he fucked me. But I was in love with him, what was there to mind? If he wanted to fuck me, I was pleased. I adore him fucking me, even if I'm not feeling incredibly horny myself. Sometimes I just lie there and let him do it to me. He knows that I love him and that I haven't gone frigid on him. He knows that I like him doing it to me even if I'm not shouting and screaming and having a hundred orgasms. He gets plenty of that, too, when I'm in the mood for it.

"He came into the kitchen the other day and I was making a salad. He put his arms around me and kissed the back of my neck and told me he loved me. Then he fondled my breasts through my sweater. My breasts are quite small, so I don't usually wear a bra. He slipped his hand up under my sweater and started to play with my nipples.

"Well, of course, by this time he was horny and I was getting a little horny, too. He said, 'Come to bed,' but I said, 'I have to finish this salad.' He lifted up my skirt at the back and slipped his hand into my pantyhose. He said, 'You *must* feel like coming to bed, your pantyhose are all wet.' I said, 'I still have to finish the salad.'

"He pulled down my pantyhose at the back, and the next thing I knew he was pushing his cock up between my legs. You know, when I think about it, so many women I know would have slapped their husbands away and said, 'Not now, not in the kitchen, can't you control yourself,' all that kind of thing.

"But I turn him on. I know that. He turns me on, too. If he wants to show me how much I turn him on by fucking me in the kitchen while I'm trying to make a salad, I'm not going to complain about that. When I'm ninety years old and I can't fuck anymore, I'd rather look back on that evening and think to myself, Well, I didn't finish the salad on time, but I was fucked. Make love, not salads, that's my motto.

"He pushed his cock right up inside me, and I was still trying to tear the lettuce. But in the end all I could do was hold on to the kitchen counter while he pushed himself up, and up, and up. He slipped his hand into the front of my pantyhose, too, and while he fucked me, he gently rolled my clitoris around with his finger, around and around, so gently I could hardly feel it.

"He came pretty quickly. Then he kissed me, squeezed me, and kissed me again, and let me get on with my salad. I didn't expect him to make me come, not then and there, although he fucked me once when I was lying out on the balcony reading a book, and I thought, He's never going to make me come, not while I'm out here reading this book. But the next thing I knew I was having one orgasm after another.

"Anyway, after he fucked me in the kitchen, I could walk around feeling all that come sliding down my leg and know for an absolute fact that the man in my life loved me. I'm not ashamed of that. I don't think it's dirty or embarrassing or anything. Men and women were made to love each other, and the more often they show it, the better, in my view. I'd much rather walk around with my panties full of my lover's come than never be loved at all.

"There are plenty of times when Andy's a little tired, or doesn't feel like playing around, and that's when I put my hand down between his legs and massage his cock for him. He always says, 'You're never going to make that hard,' but I always do. It wouldn't upset me, even if I didn't. I just enjoy the feeling of rubbing and massaging his cock. I love it when it grows really stiff in my hand, then I rub it up and down really slowly, and then at last starts to ooze out a little slippery juice, crystal-clear, and I slide that up and down his cock and massage his balls with it, too.

"I can always tell when he's just about to come; he really tightens up his muscles and he grips my arm. Then I rub him very, very slowly, until he's so tensed up that he's begging me to rub him harder and faster. But I won't. I do it slowly and gently, until I can feel his cock bulging. Then I grip it really hard, right down at the base of it, and his come shoots out everywhere. I love to feel it shooting out.

"Maybe that's all we'll do. I don't necessarily expect him to make me come in return, although he often does, because he feels like it. Either he masturbates me with his fingers, or else he goes down on me and licks me with his tongue. He can do that for hours, as far as I'm concerned. I just adore the feeling of it, even when I don't think that I'm ever going to come.

"Other times, I'll masturbate myself and let him watch me. But by the time I'm halfway through doing that, he's usually raring to fuck me in any case. But I don't think that a couple should always think that they both have to be satisfied at one and the same time. Sometimes I lie in bed next to Andy and masturbate. I make no secret of what I'm doing. It doesn't mean that he doesn't satisfy me. It simply means that I like masturbating, it's a good feeling.

"How would I feel if Andy masturbated? Just the same. I couldn't be jealous of my husband's own left hand, could I? But if he felt like masturbating, I'd prefer it if he fucked me instead, even if I didn't feel like it too much. Yes, I'd have to say that. Just selfish, I guess."

It's startlingly apparent when you talk to happy and well-satisfied couples that they speak about their sexual techniques and the intimate details of their sex lives with very little shame. They relish their sexual happiness, and they relish everything that they find exciting, from full-blown scenarios of passionate intercourse to the tiniest erotic gesture. They enjoy each other's bodies and they delight in each other's pleasure, and if one of them happens to find out that the other's climax is intensified by some particular technique, they are rarely too shy to discuss it or to share it.

So many other women score over wives by being prepared to talk about sex and special sexual desires. "My wife doesn't understand me" isn't by any means the commonest complaint in marriages that are under stress. The slogan I hear most frequently from disaffected husbands is, "I've always wanted to try this (or that, or the other), but I wouldn't ever ask my wife to do it." Or maybe they have asked, and been refused.

This is Katherine, a twenty-nine-year-old secretary for a large petroleum corporation in Houston, Texas. Katherine has never married ("never felt the need"), but she has had seven major affairs, five of them with married men, and some "not-so-major" affairs. At the time I talked to her, she was living alone "for a while, anyhow."

What did Katherine think that most men found lacking in their married sex lives? Was it variety?

"I don't think that men are as worried about variety and novelty as people like to think. I've had wives on the phone and they've said to me, 'What is it about you that my husband prefers? What do you do for him that I don't?'

"For sure, most married men are excited by sleeping with a different woman after six or seven years of sleeping with the same one. Just lying next to a different body must be something of a turn-on.

"I'm always willing to try anything. I have no sexual inhibitions except that I don't like the idea of a man tying me up. It's never happened to me and I don't want it to happen to me. It's not my idea of a good time. I don't like the idea of deliberate pain, either, although sometimes it can be exciting to have your nipples bitten or your back scratched, just so long as it happens in the heat of the moment. I don't like the idea of cold-blooded sadism.

"What most married men seem to want is relaxed, free-and-easy sex. They like oral sex very much. They like to have their penises sucked and they like to suck my pussy in return. They like having sex in different places. On the rug, maybe, in front of the fire. They must find it stimulating simply to be having sex someplace else apart from their own familiar king-size at home. They don't go for anal sex very much. I enjoy anal sex—there aren't many sensations in the world to compare with having a huge stiff penis up your ass—but I know that quite a lot of women don't go for it at all, they positively hate it, and I find that particularly among married women. They think that it diminishes their dignity, or something like that. But anyway they don't care for it.

"Most of the time I find that what my married lovers wanted was quantity, rather than quality. They simply wanted a lot more sex than they were getting. And they didn't ease up, either, as the months went by.

"Men have this very immediate sexual appetite; it's like they feel hungry suddenly and they want to be fed there and then. With women it's different; they like a sexual relationship to be romantic, they like to be persuaded into bed. I like romance, and believe me, I get a lot of romance. Married men can be very romantic, wonderfully considerate, much more than single men. They've had all the arrogance knocked out of them. They know how to take a woman out and make her feel like a woman. They care.

"But I'm not stupid enough to think that any sexual relationship can be all one-sided. Men and woman have different sexual needs; somehow they have to make the effort to satisfy each other, they have to make concessions, they have to make compromises. A man has to wine and dine the woman in his life, he has to buy her flowers and tell her she's beautiful. A woman sometimes has to behave like a whore and be prepared to have sex like *now*, drag down your panties, open your legs, thrust it in.

"When men and women start getting inside of each other's heads, start understanding each other sexually, then marriages are going to be sexier and last longer, and girls like me are going to have to start looking elsewhere."

Katherine said that her most startling sexual experience was when she and her married lover were surprised at her apartment by the man's wife.

"By complete coincidence, she had been driving past and seen David parking outside my apartment. She had suspected for three or four months that David had been sleeping with another woman, so of course she stopped her car and followed him up to my apartment.

"David was always very fierce and impetuous with me. The second I opened the door, he wanted to make love to me there and then. He used to carry me into the bedroom with my legs twined around him, and he used to drag off my pantyhose and make love to me really roughly, almost like he was raping me. After that, we used to lie on the bed together and have a drink. Then I used to start fondling him and kissing him and sucking his penis, until he got hard again. Then I would sit on top of him and make love to him very slowly. That was the way it happened almost every time. That was the way he liked it.

"This time, though, we were making furious love on the bed when the doorbell rang. David told me to ignore it, but I was expecting a gown from the cleaners, so I broke off and went to answer it. And there, of course, was Sally, David's wife.

"I thought, Oh, God, now the ceiling's going to fall in. But it didn't. She came into my apartment very quietly, and she said, 'I know what's been going on. I know that you and David have been sleeping together. I want to know why.'

"David was in the bedroom naked. Sally went straight through and said, 'Why, David? What has Katherine got that I haven't got? What can Katherine do for you that I can't do? I want to learn.'

"Right in front of us, she unbuttoned her blouse, unfastened her skirt, and stepped out of her panties. David said, 'Sally, for God's sake.' But she was determined. She climbed onto the bed, completely naked, except for her really expensive wristwatch and a gold chain around her ankle, and she said, 'Show me. Come on. Show me what you do.'

"I didn't know how to react. I didn't know whether to walk right out of the place, or what. But then David said, 'All right, Sally, if that's the way you want it.' And he beckoned me onto the bed, and I thought, Oh, well, what the hell. And I came.

"David was lying on his back on the bed. I knelt one side of him and Sally knelt on the other. I took his penis in my hand and gently started to massage it, until it stiffened up, and then I kissed it and licked it and took it into my mouth. I knew from what David had told me that Sally had never given him oral sex. But now she bent forward, too, and while I was sucking the head of his penis, she started licking the shaft of it. Then we were both sucking the head, our lips pressed together with his stiff penis in both of our mouths, both licking at it and licking at each other's tongues, too.

"We hardly needed to say anything. Sally carried on sucking his penis while I took his balls into my mouth, one after the other. David was practically out of his mind, with two women sucking his penis at the same time. I told Sally, 'Get on top of him, make love to him.' But she shook her head and said, 'You do it. I want to see how you do it.'

"So I climbed on top of him, and Sally took hold of his penis and pushed it up inside my pussy with her hand. We made love real slow, that beautiful long rocking-horse rhythm, and all the time we were doing that, Sally was fondling and massaging David's penis and my pussy.

"The feeling was absolutely sensational. I've never felt anything like it before or since. To have another woman fondling you while you're making love . . . I must have had dozens and dozens of tiny little popping climaxes, they wouldn't stop.

"Toward the end, Sally pushed her fingers into my pussy, alongside of David's penis, and gently scratched him with her fingernails. He climaxed like a thunderbolt, believe me. His penis came out of me, and I swear his come was spurting right up in the air. Some if it landed on my shoulder and some on Sally's breasts.

"After it was all over, Sally said to David, 'Are you coming home now? There's nothing you can get here that you can't get at home.'

"David looked at me and I knew what he was thinking. I said, 'Go on, sweetheart. Back where you belong.'

"And so he did."

8

How to Be His Other Woman

We have explored the innermost reaches of what men find sexually stimulating ... and what they find lacking in their day-to-day sexual relationships. We have seen how your fresh new positive approach to your sex life can ensure that your man is both excited and satisfied in bed.

We have seen how you can satisfy sexual urges that he may not even have been consciously aware that he had.

But the appeal of the "other woman" is more than her willingness to satisfy particular sexual urges. You may be ready to satisfy his craving for oral sex or masturbation. You may be more than happy to join him in bed with an erotic video movie and all the chocolates you can eat.

But the reason why so many men go looking for another woman is not entirely sexual. All of the straying husbands I talked to when I researched this book said that the women for whom they had left their wives had one strong overriding quality about them.

They were not only sexually interested in them; they were interested in everything they did and everything they said. A large part of their erotic appeal was that they made the men feel like men again—characterful, interesting, and masculine, not just husbands or fathers or breadwinners.

"I fell for Judy because she made me feel sexy again," said thirty-eight-year-old Brad, the vice-president of a computer company in Silicon Valley. "She was fascinated by my job; she wanted to learn how computers worked. She was interested in my golfing. She came along to the opera with me, which Brenda had never done, not once. I hadn't just found a mistress; I had found a soul mate."

I heard the same story again and again. Not only had the "other women" scored by being more adventurous and more positive in bed; they had scored by showing that what mattered to their lovers mattered to them, too—even if it was something as mundane as golf.

"Tina is a friend that I have sex with," explained thirty-four-year-old Newton, a store manager from Fresno. "I always think about her as a friend first, and a lover second. If my dick was accidentally chopped off, God forbid, we'd still be friends."

Another plus for other women was that they invariably made sure that they were well-groomed and well-dressed. While it is obviously more difficult for a wife to surprise her husband with new clothes and new hairstyles, it isn't at all difficult for her to look at herself in the mirror now and again and check that she hasn't become frowzy and staid.

A few seconds spent grooming herself will pay tremendous dividends in terms of sexual attractiveness, as well as making her feel more feminine. Here's Jacqueline, a twenty-eight-year-old homemaker and mother from Los Angeles, "After Gary was born, I became completely preoccupied with the two children and the house. I loved having those children and I loved my home, and all the time I didn't notice that I was becoming a complete frump. I used to slop around the place in an old T-shirt and baggy jeans. I didn't bother about my hair, I used to tie it back in a ponytail and that was it. My nails were all broken, I didn't bother to wax my legs or anything.

"Our sex life wasn't up to much, either, because I was always too tired after baking or painting the house or playing with the children. When Gary was about seven months old, a friend of mine called me and said that she'd seen Donald in Westwood with some redheaded woman, and she thought I ought to know about it because they had been holding hands and looking really cozy together.

"I was thrown totally off-balance. Up until then, I'd really believed that our marriage was perfect. I thought about confronting Donald with it at first, you know, having a showdown. But I talked to another friend of mine who'd been divorced when she was twenty-two, and she said that the last thing I ought to do was to act antagonistic. She said it didn't matter how bad I felt about Donald, the reason he was dating another woman was because I wasn't what he wanted anymore. She said, 'Go on, take stock of yourself,' and so I did.

"It's quite a shock when you look at yourself objectively like that, when you ask yourself, 'Do men find me sexy? Do they find me even remotely attractive?' I looked at myself and I couldn't believe what I had allowed myself to turn into, I just couldn't. I was never one of those fussy girls who paints their toenails every day or anything like that. But my hair always used to be well-cut and colored and washed, and I always used to have a little eye makeup on. But the woman who was looking back at me out of the mirror had about as much sex appeal as a raw carrot. I looked tired, scrubbed, and shapeless.

"At first I thought, What the hell, this is me; if he doesn't like me this way, that's too bad. But that wasn't being fair on him and it sure as hell wasn't being fair on me, either. I was on the point of losing my husband because I was looking so dowdy, because I wasn't taking any pride in my appearance anymore.

"For all I knew, I might have lost him already.

"Well, that afternoon I left the children with a sitter, and I went and fixed my hair and had a manicure at the same time. On the way back from the beauty parlor, I stopped off and bought some new underwear. It was expensive—Swiss, most of it—but it was very chic and very sexy. My favorite was this little peach-colored bikini with shell patterns embroidered on it. I said to the assistant, 'It sure doesn't cover much. Surely that's the kind of thing that strippers wear?' But she said that all the dressiest women wear bikini panties these days, especially underneath slacks, that's why they're all so beautifully embroidered—nothing like the old Frederick's of Hollywood-type G-string.

"I bought myself a silk blouse and a mini-skirt, too. Then I went back home and I sprayed myself with Donald's favorite perfume.

"He couldn't believe it when he got home. He just stood and stared at me and said, 'What's happened to you?' I told him the truth. Well, most of the truth. I said that I'd taken a good long look at myself and suddenly realized that I wasn't the girl he had married anymore. He couldn't keep his eyes off me all evening, and when the children had gone to bed, he went out to the liquor store and bought us a bottle of Chandon Brut.

"We sat in front of the fire and drank champagne, and it was just like we were courting all over again. He kissed me like he hadn't kissed me for years. But then I pushed him gently back on the cushions and I unbuttoned his shirt, and then I opened up his pants, too, and took out his cock.

"I'd never done that before, not so blatantly, but I knew that I had to take the initiative or else the chances were that I was going to lose him. I kissed the top of his cock and it tasted all salty and delicious, the way that a man's cock always does. Then I licked it all the way down, right down to his balls, and then I took his balls into my mouth, one after the other, like they were plums.

"Then I opened my mouth wide and took the head of his cock right into my mouth, flicking the underneath of it with my tongue, probing my tongue right into that little hole. Then I gently sucked him and rubbed him with my hand and tried to act like an expert hooker, you know?

"He was all stiff and uncertain to begin with. I don't think he could really believe what was happening. I'd never sucked his cock before, not like this, although I'd kissed it once or twice. But now I was giving him the whole business, you know, slowly sucking it up and down, pushing it right into my cheek, rubbing it all around my face.

"After a while he couldn't hold it anymore. He lifted up my skirt, and when he discovered my panties, he said something like, 'Jesus, you sexy lady.' He lifted me up. He's a whole lot physically bigger than I am, and he opened up my pussy with his fingers, and he lowered me down onto his cock, slow and slippery and beautiful. Then he lifted me up and down, up and down, and after only about the fourth time he came. I could actually feel his cock bulging as it came out—at least I thought I could.

"I slid down him again and took his cock back into my mouth, sucking out the last of his sperm and licking off my own juice.

"We made love twice more that night and once before Donald went off to work in the morning. I let him do anything he wanted. I'd never liked him touching my anus very much, but that night I let him push two fingers right up it. He didn't hurt me, not at all, and he didn't do anything kinky. But he made love to me again and again, and that was fantastic. It brought us together, that night, like you wouldn't believe it. It was like the first night we met, all over again. Action replay.

"I never found out what happened to the redhead. It could be that there never was anything between them. You know how business people kiss and call each other 'darling,' and it doesn't mean a thing. But even if there wasn't any redhead, what I did that night was long overdue. You can't expect your husband to be faithful and turned on if you don't show him that you *care* about yourself and your marriage and the way you look. Of course, looks aren't everything, and toenail varnish isn't everything, but showing you care, that's what's important. Showing you're a woman and that you're still interested in arousing your man."

Donna, a twenty-three-year-old personnel assistant for an avionics corporation in Salt Lake City, Utah, used her natural friendliness and her interest in other people to win her thirty-seven-year-old boss, Leonard, away from his wife. Brunette, vivacious, with a figure that wouldn't disgrace a *Playboy* centerfold, Donna believes that "the only moral criterion in human relationships is happiness. I think misery is indefensible."

Whatever you think of her personal philosophy, she won Leonard's affections by taking a genuine interest in his pet subject, the history of World War Two.

"When I first met Leonard, my reaction was, Wow! What a good-looking guy! A little too old for me, I guess, but he had that beautiful sad Frank Langella look about him. I didn't make too much of a pitch for him at first. One of my friends at the office told me that he was married with two kids and that he never fooled around, not even at the Christmas party. But the more I got to know him, the more I began to feel that he was sad and frustrated and unhappy.

"One night we were working late, and I asked him if he was happy. He was kind of surprised that I asked him so direct, but he took me to a bar after we were all finished, and we talked some more. He didn't give much away, believe me. He was very loyal to his wife. But the more he talked, the more I realized that he was utterly depressed. He didn't love his wife at all. He liked her, for sure. I think he still does. But there was no spark there, you know what I mean? In fact, I don't believe he *ever* loved her, not even when they were first married.

"After a while he started talking about World War Two. His pet subject. He'd made an amazing study of it, he told me all about the fall of Berlin, and the Führerbunker, and how Hitler and Eva Braun had died. It was totally fascinating. He made it come to life. Then he said, 'I'd better shut up, I'm boring you.' But I said, 'No, of course you're not, it's amazing. It's better than watching it on television.'

"He didn't believe me. He really didn't believe me. And the reason he didn't believe me was because his wife had never listened to him and never taken an interest. It was his one big hobby, and even if she did find it boring, she had a duty to listen to what he was saying, at least—just as much as he had a duty to listen to anything that she had to say.

"At that time I didn't think that I was going to have an affair with Leonard. I thought we would probably be friends, nothing more. He took me for drinks; we went for walks at lunchtime when the weather was good, and brown-bagged it. I suppose I knew that we were falling in love, but it seemed so pleasant and so natural; it was so much a part of our friendship that when he asked me to go on a business trip with him to Albuquerque, I guess I just said yes, even though I knew then that we were going to sleep together.

"There was one thing I knew about Leonard's wife. She was a mature-minded woman, very capable. Leonard liked that maturity in one way; it meant that she could take care of his accounts and look after the house. But in another way he didn't like it at all. Capability isn't sexy, if you know what I mean. Sometimes men like a woman who's a little dippy, a little defenseless, a kind of a Marilyn Monroe scatterbrain. It makes them feel more virile, and believe me, I'm all for that.

"When we went to Albuquerque, I wore a very tight red dress and curled my hair, and I made sure that I looked really sexy and breathy and dizzy. On the plane I told Leonard that I'd forgotten to pack any underwear, so if we had time maybe he could help me choose some—or if not, I wouldn't bother to wear any. It was a pretty obvious ploy, but it was so different from anything that his wife would have done. I said, 'I even forgot to put any panties on today.'

"Well, of course, that started his motor running, and it didn't stop all the way to the hotel. As soon as the bellman had left our room and Leonard had locked the door, he took me in his arms and kissed me, and then he just had to lift up my dress to run his hands all over my naked bottom. I'd shaved off all of my pubic hair, too, so that I looked little-girlish, and he cupped my bare cunt in his hand and I swear that he closed his eyes and said a prayer.

"He laid me on the bed and tore off his clothes so quickly that he ripped the sleeve of his shirt. He got on top of me and pushed my thighs apart with his knees, and all I could see was that big purple cock he was holding in his fist. He pushed it straight up inside me, and he fucked me like a man who hasn't had sex for twenty years. Wild, furious, like he was trying to make up for all of those years he'd missed.

"I never once asked him to leave his wife and children, but in the end he said that he couldn't live without me, and so he did. It was his decision, but I won't say that I put any obstacles in his way. I tried to show an interest in everything he did: his hobbies and his jokes and his funny ideas. I let him teach me how to ski, even though I hate the snow and I never liked the idea of skiing at all. And I tried always to understand what he wanted in bed.

"He likes me to sit astride his chest, facing away from him, so that I can slowly rub his cock stiff with my hand. Then he likes me to push my fanny gradually backward, so that he can lick my cunt. He does it beautifully slowly, his tongue works all the way around, and he won't even touch my clitoris until I'm more than ready, even though sometimes he's turning me on so much that I feel like screaming at him.

"When he starts licking my clitoris, he does it really quickly until I have an orgasm, and while I'm still having my orgasm, he rolls me over on the bed and pushes his cock into me. That gives me orgasms that literally go on and on and on, and won't stop.

"Another thing he likes is for me to wear a sweater and long woolen stockings in bed, and gloves, so that only my bottom and my cunt are bare. I found out about that when we were skiing at Squaw Valley. I was dressing, and he saw me standing by the mirror wearing these long woolen stockings and a sweater and nothing else, and even though there wasn't time for us to do anything then, he said, 'My God, you're gorgeous,' and I knew that it really lit his fire.

"Sometimes I think that wives don't listen enough to flattery. Their husband will say something like, 'I really like you in that skirt, or dress, or whatever,' and all they ever do is say, 'This old thing? Don't be silly.' They're making the double mistake of squelching his ego by telling him not to be silly; and at the same time they're missing the point that when a man says, 'I really like you in that skirt,' he's paying you a genuine compliment that means, 'You really look sexy and feminine in that skirt and you turn me on.'

"I don't feel guilty about taking Leonard away from his family, mainly because I didn't take him away. He left his wife and children because he was unhappy, because he needed a much more satisfying sex life, because he wanted somebody to understand him. You know that old thing, 'My wife doesn't understand me.' It may be a cliché, but a lot of the time I think it's true. Wives have forgotten how to listen, they've forgotten how to flirt. Just because you've been living with a man for fifteen years, that doesn't mean you don't have to flutter your eyelashes and waggle your fanny from time to time."

Sophie, thirty-one, from Portland, Oregon, lost her husband, Jim, to his secretary, Paula, a vivacious blonde. But she got him back by refusing to admit defeat and setting out to have an affair with him.

"The odd part about it was that when Jim told me he was sleeping with Paula and that he wanted to leave me, I wasn't at all surprised. I surprised myself because I was so unsurprised. I knew that our sex life hadn't been at all interesting, not for a couple of years, and when I first saw Paula, I actually thought to myself, That's the kind of girl who could turn Jim on.

"But when he actually packed his valise and left, actually walked out of the door, then it hit me what had happened. And I thought to myself, I'm standing here like an idiot and I'm letting that girl walk off with my husband, *my* husband! I'm allowing her to break up a marriage in which I happen to have invested fourteen years of my life, and I'm not even raising my voice. It was unbelievable!

"At first I didn't know what to do. I called Jim at work, but most of the time he wouldn't talk to me, and when he did, he accused me of being dreary and depressed. Well, of course I was dreary and depressed. But one day, when I was waiting to talk to him on the phone, I heard Paula laughing, and Jim laughing, too; and it suddenly occurred to me that abandoned wives don't do themselves any good at all by acting so sorry for themselves all of the time. The more dreary and depressed they sound, the less attractive they are.

"I thought, Paula's bright and sexy and fun, and that's what I'm going to be. I went out and bought all the books on sex that I could find—*The Joy of Sex* and *How to Drive Your Man Wild in Bed*—and I found out then just how much I didn't know about sex. It was an eye-opener. I hadn't even known where my clitoris was or how it worked, or the best way to hold a man's penis, or how to stop a man from coming if he started coming too soon.

"I invited Jim to come around after work one day, just to talk about divorce. I wasn't miserable. I wasn't hysterical. I dressed up sexily, but not too sexily. I didn't want to look as if I was making too much of a play for him. A short skirt and a tight sweater. Something he hadn't seen me wearing before, so that he'd realize that, even after he'd left me, my life was still going on.

"We talked for a while about going to see an attorney, and then I said, 'Could you do one thing for me? Could you make love to me one last time?'

"I kissed him and gripped his penis through his slacks, and I knew that he wasn't going to say no. After all, we were still married, and it was pretty flattering for him to think that two women both wanted to make love to him.

"We went into the bedroom and I undressed him first. I'd worked that out for myself, undressing him first. I think it was important because once he was naked he was committed, whereas if I'd undressed first, he might suddenly have had a pang of conscience about Paula and changed his mind. After all, whatever I thought about it, Paula was the one that he had chosen, out of the two of us.

"I took off my sweater and my skirt, but I kept on my stockings and my garter belt. I pushed Jim back onto the bed and kissed him, and then I kissed him all the way down his chest and squeezed and massaged his penis in between my breasts. He reached down and tried to pull me up again, so that he could make love to me, but I wouldn't let him, not right away. I pushed his legs open wide and I kissed his penis and his balls. Then I wet my finger by dipping it into my vagina, making sure that he could see what I was doing, and I slowly pushed it up his ass, sharp fingernail and all, right up to the knuckle.

"At the same time I licked his penis the way a cat licks cream, right from the bottom to the top, giving the top a really long suck right at the end. He actually moaned out loud. I don't think he could believe what was happening to him. And with me, his wife—the wife whom he was thinking of leaving.

"I went on kissing him and licking him, then when I could taste the first slippery juice coming out of him, I turned over on my back and opened my legs up for him. He made love to me then like he'd never made love to me before, because he was doing it the way I wanted him to do it. I wouldn't let him rush, I wouldn't let him finish too quickly, and it was fantastic. He really satisfied me, and he knew that he'd satisfied me. And because of that, he felt real good about it.

"We went on seeing each other, even though he was living with Paula. He used to tell her that he had to meet me to talk about the divorce, about alimony, about selling the house, but every time he came to see me, we used to make love.

"I guess it was kind of strange, having an affair with your own husband, but after the third or fourth time that Jim came around to see me, I knew that I was going to get him back. I wanted him back. I loved him. I knew that neither of us had put everything into our marriage that we should have done. So there was room for improvement. I guess there always is, in any relationship.

"One evening he came around to see me on his way back from work, and when he arrived, I made sure that I was completely naked. He asked me 'What's going on? Why are you nude?' I said, 'I'm living on my own now. Why should I worry about dressing?'

"That was the night he stayed all night, and when it was morning, he said he wanted to stay permanently, he wanted us to stay married.

"Even then I didn't push him. I didn't tell him that he had to tell Paula immediately that everything was off. I told him to go to work and think about it, and if he wanted to come back, well, then, he was welcome.

"Of course, I spent all day biting my nails—worrying if he was really going to come back or not.

But at six P.M., there he was, with a huge bouquet of flowers and a bottle of champagne, and I knew that I'd won him back.

"I don't feel that I prostituted myself in any way, no. Why should I? He's my husband, he and I should have been closer. We should have been better friends, as well as sexually closer. I don't think that it's ever too late to improve your marriage, and if one partner has to flirt with the other partner to do it, well, that's the name of the game.

"To begin with, yes, I did think I was acting like a whore. But, do you know something, if you act like a whore with your husband you get all the excitement of being a whore and yet all the loyalty of being married, too. I recommend it."

Apart from sex, Sophie mentioned another factor that has always struck me as crucial in any relationship: a sense of fun and a sense of laughter. I sometimes wonder how many girls have won husbands away from wives simply because of their gaiety and their ability to laugh.

Being married and being responsible for a family is a serious business, which doesn't do much for anybody's sense of humor, and when a man meets a girl with whom he can giggle, he is often attracted to her more for that reason than anything else.

"When Frank and I broke up and I asked him why, he said, 'You never laugh, you're always so damned serious!'

"I was angry, but it was true. I wasn't any fun anymore. All I was thinking about was running the home, staying slim, making sure that the kids got to school on time, paying the bills. And then some young girl comes along who doesn't care about anything except when she's going to wash her hair . . . Of course, a man is going to find her attractive.

"When a man is unfaithful to his wife, more often than not, in my opinion, he's being unfaithful not so much to his wife as a person, but to the responsibility of being married to her. Taking care of a family, that's heavy responsibility. So, for just a moment, when some laughing young girl appears in his life, he's reminded of all those times when he didn't have to worry about a mortgage, or dental fees, or baby-sitters . . . and a wife has her work cut out, trying to compete with somebody like that."

There will always be men who will never settle down, who will duck out from responsibility whenever it becomes too tedious or too onerous. But most men will accept their responsibilities gladly, provided that the fun continues and that they still get the sexual excitement that made your relationship great to begin with.

We've already seen how you can continue to excite the man in your life, how you can find out what his secret urges and fantasies are, and how you can satisfy them. But you should never forget to laugh. You should never take yourself too seriously. You may be worried about credit repayments, or just how much it's going to cost you to send the children to camp this summer, but try to lighten up. Your man remembers the laughing, sparkling you that you were when you very first met him. Don't let him go looking for that vivacious young lady in somebody else.

My philosophy—based on twenty-two years of study as a sexual counselor—is that you should always try to think of yourself as the other woman, as the woman who is trying to take your husband away from somebody else. Be a lover, be a friend, be a mistress, and never shy away from any sexual act that makes you both feel more excited.

"I went to a party with my husband Philip," said thirty-three-year-old Norma from Madison, Wisconsin. "He spent all evening talking to a very pretty dark-haired girl in a bright-red dress. She seemed very witty and confident, and I have to admit that I was jealous. I was talking to a friend of mine, and I asked her who the girl was. She said, 'What girl?' and I said, 'The girl that Philip seems to be so interested in.' She said, 'Oh—the girl who looks just like you.'

"Now that came as a shock. But I suddenly realized she was right. The girl did look like me. Only she looked the way I used to look when I was first courting Philip and I was bright and funny and vivacious and when I really cared about dressing to attract him.

"Believe me, I had been thinking about giving Philip a hard time for spending all evening talking to this one girl, but I thought to myself, Learn your lesson. Make sure that he wants to talk to you instead.

"I changed my hairstyle, I bought some clothes, I spent some time grooming myself. I also went back to reading newspapers and magazines and picking up bits and pieces of interesting information, the way I always used to before I was married. I bought some sexy new nightdresses, too, not sleazy, but really beautiful silk. Philip's the kind of man who likes his sex classy, if you know what I mean.

"When he came home that weekend, I made sure that I was ready for him. I bought two bottles of good red wine and two steaks, and I had music playing and a fire burning, and I was wearing this ivory silk negligee, and underneath it a matching nightdress that left my breasts completely bare.

"I don't think Philip knew what had hit him, but he liked it. In fact, he loved it. I slipped off the negligee and kissed him and gave him a glass of wine, but believe me he didn't want the glass of wine. He laid me straight down on the couch and stripped off his business suit and his shirt and his shorts, and he had an erection like a great stiff red rod.

"He kissed me and kissed my breasts, and then he couldn't hold himself back any longer. He lifted my legs over his shoulders and he pushed that great stiff red rod right up me, and he made love to me.

"We made love twice before dinner and once afterward and again during the night. It was fantastic; it was just like our honeymoon all over again.

And what was so incredible about it was that I hadn't done anything particularly special. I'd just tried to make myself as vivacious as the girl at the party, so that Philip would pay me the same kind of attention."

The effect of Norma's new approach was permanent. After that night, she found that her relationship with Philip was much closer, much more effervescent, much sexier, and much more fun for both of them.

But isn't it demeaning for women to dress themselves up as sex objects and behave like whores with their own husbands just to get the sexual response that should be theirs by right?

"I believe in women being equal, but I also believe in women being feminine. That's the excitement of sex, being totally feminine, seeing the influence that you have over your husband's responses. To be able to excite and satisfy your husband, even after ten years of marriage, that's quite an achievement, and I can't see how any woman can think of it as demeaning."

Of course, revitalizing your sex life isn't solely your responsibility. Your husband or lover can do a great deal to relight those fireworks, too, as I have described in *How to Be the Perfect Lover* and *How to Drive Your Woman Wild in Bed.* But if your sex life is flagging and your mate isn't doing much to revive it, then it's up to you to start acting in a way that will stir him up.

Charlene, twenty-eight, from Baton Rouge, Louisiana, said, "Jack and I had been going through some pretty bad times, mainly because of money worries. We were making love only once in a blue moon, and because of that, we were both frustrated, aruging almost every night and drinking too much; things got to such a point that I began to believe that the only answer was for us to break up.

"But a girlfriend of mine was talking to me, and she said that on the weekend she never got dressed, except when she went out shopping. Maybe she'd wear a short T-shirt or a pair of sox or a couple of bracelets or just a beret or something, but otherwise she made the breakfast and she tidied up the house completely nude. She said her husband went crazy for it. He loved it. She had sex so many times over the weekend that she stayed in bed late on Monday morning, just to get over it, and she'd been married for nearly seven years.

"When I told her how bad things were between me and Jack, she said I should try it. She said I should depilate my vagina, that would make his eyes stand out and his cock stick up, and that I should do everything nude, except for some small decoration like maybe a neck scarf. She said the decoration had the effect of making you look nuder than nude.

"What can I tell you? I went home and shaved myself; the I put on three big turquoise-and-silver Indian necklaces Jack had brought me back from Arizona, and that's how I looked when Jack came home and found me making his supper.

"He asked me what the hell I was doing, and all I said was, 'It's time you had a wife who was a whole lot sexier.' He said, 'Well, that's for sure.' He thought it was incredible, just incredible. He took me to bed right away and we spent over an hour in bed, making love. Afterward he asked me if I was going to be dressed, but I said no. Tonight I was going to stay nude all night, just for him.

"I finished making the supper in the nude, and afterward I washed the dishes in the nude, with Jack's come sliding down the insides of my thighs. He came right up behind me and made love to me again, standing at the sink."

Again and again, I have been told of examples where a simple breakthrough in sexual intimacy has worked wonders in every aspect of a stale marriage. Where a wife has set aside her shyness and her reserve and has flirted with her husband as if she were the other woman.

All you need is the determination to make your

marriage sparkle—and the confidence to behave in a really sexy way.

Taking that first step isn't easy. What's my husband going to think? is the anxious question that most wives ask. He's going to think there's something wrong.

But you'll be surprised how positive and immediate his response is and the dividends that your sexual investment will eventually pay you.

The adventure can be yours. Why not start out on it tonight?

9

50 Things
That Other Women Do
to Please Their Men

Here are some of the favorite sexual ways in which the other woman excites the man who has come into her life.

1) By opening his pants and fondling him while he drives his car.
2) By taking out his penis and giving him oral sex even before he has time to hang up his hat.
3) By masturbating him while he watches football on TV.
4) By sucking his penis first thing in the morning, while he is still asleep.
5) By walking around the house nude.
6) By lying back and spreading their thighs while they are sitting on a couch or armchair, and making it clear that she relishes her lover's look-and-fondle curiosity.
7) By asking him to give her oral sex while she's sunbathing (she simply slips that bathing costume to one side and makes sure that she massages his back with suntan lotion while's he's lapping away).
8) By giving him a scented-oil massage . . . climaxing in very slow masturbation.
9) By wearing stockings and garter belt to bed.
10) By wearing high-heeled shoes to bed.
11) By asking him more about his business, and being interested when he tells her.

12) By sliding her finger up his anus while he makes love to her.
13) By telling him he's the most exciting lover she ever had.
14) By giving him oral sex and swallowing his semen.
15) By giving him oral sex and then aiming his climaxing penis over her breasts.
16) By wearing erotic underwear.
17) By wearing no underwear at all and making it obvious (to him, anyway).
18) By suggesting he makes love to her at just about any time of the day except bedtime.
19) By coaxing him into anal sex.
20) By scratching his back and biting his neck when she makes love—except if this is an illicit affair, in which case he certainly won't want to return home to his wife carrying his battle scars.
21) By dressing up in rubberwear.
22) By masturbating while he watches.
23) By making love to him in the tub or the shower—or the swimming pool or the Jacuzzi, or the sauna.
24) By caressing his penis with her toes.
25) By reading sexy magazines with him and trying to imitate the action.
26) By sliding a humming vibrator up her anus while he makes love to her.
27) By sliding a humming vibrator up her vagina while he penetrates her anally.
28) By greeting him at the front door wearing absolutely nothing.
29) By dressing beautifully for him, so that his friends and his colleagues are impressed and attracted by his stunning companion.
30) By waxing her legs, manicuring her nails, making up her eyes, and always making sure that she looks immaculate.
31) By being witty, lighthearted, and well-informed.

32) By slowly undressing him before he undresses her.
33) By giving him intimate and provocative glimpses of herself (in the bathroom mirror, through a half-open door, lying asleep in bed).
34) By inventing sexy outfits for herself (scarves, ribbons, tight shorts with the crotch cut out of them).
35) By shaving her pubic hair.
36) By taking videos of herself naked while he's at work and showing them to him when he returns home.
37) By taking videos of their lovemaking and watching them with him while they make love yet again.
38) By talking dirty to him while she makes love.
39) By describing her most erotic fantasy to him, in delicious detail.
40) By asking him what his most erotic fantasy is and then embellishing it with sexy suggestions of her own.
41) By masturbating him through his pants pockets at parties, or the racetrack, or anyplace else exciting and different.
42) By telling him what he can do to make himself look more attractive.
43) By showing her what turns her on the most.
44) By demonstrating exactly how she likes to have her clitoris fondled.
45) By massaging his penis with her hair.
46) By encouraging him to watch her while she urinates.
47) By asking him to masturbate her while she urinates.
48) By masturbating him while fully dressed and then guiding his penis so that he ejaculates inside her tugged-open panties

—and then wearing them wet for the rest of the day.

49) By learning as much about sex and sexual responses as she possibly can ... and putting that knowledge into constant practice. After all, practice makes perfect.

50) By always treating her man as if he is the very best lover that ever was.

About the Author

GRAHAM MASTERTON, forty-two years old, is the author of four of the best-selling sexual manuals of all time, *How to Drive Your Man Wild in Bed,* *How to Be the Perfect Lover, More Ways to Drive Your Man Wild in Bed,* and *How to Drive Your Woman Wild in Bed.* A former editor of *Mayfair, Penthouse,* and *Forum* magazines, he now divides his time between his researches in the United States and his home in Epsom, England. He is married, and has three sons.